THE WONDER OF YORK MINSTER

Published by
Cerialis Press, York. ©
Printed by Herald Printers, (Westminster Press Ltd.), York and London.

Dr. Bernard M. Feilden
with a group of important individuals who were largely responsible
in their various activities for the restoration of York Minster.

(*Left to right*): David Chapman—Resident Engineer—*Ove Arup & Partners* (*Consulting Engineers*). David Mitchell—Research Engineer—*Ove Arup & Partners* (*Consulting Engineers*). Kenneth Stephens—Construction Manager—*Shepherd Construction Limited*. David Dowrick—Project Engineer—*Ove Arup & Partners* (*Consulting Engineers*). Frank Hall—Quantity Surveyor—*Ashley Cooper Hall* (*Quantity Surveyors*). Dr. Bernard M. Feilden, C.B.E.—Surveyor of Fabric (*Feilden & Mawson Architects*). Christopher Richmond—Superintendent of Works—*Dean and Chapter, York Minster*. Frank Berry—*York Minster Appeal Fund*. Herman Ramm—Archaeologist—*Royal Commission on Historical Monuments*. Derek Phillips—Archaeologist. Director of Excavations—*Dean and Chapter, York Minster*.

THE WONDER OF YORK MINSTER

by

DR. BERNARD M. FEILDEN,
CBE, FSA, FRSA, AA Dipl(Hons), RIBA

with an Introduction

by

The Dean of York, The Very Reverend Ronald Jasper,
MA, DD, FR Hist S

CONTENTS

INTRODUCTION

WHEN I first read the manuscript of this book, I was a little perplexed about the title. It seemed to me that something like "The Rescue of York Minster" might be more appropriate: at least it would provide a clear indication of its contents. But the more I looked at the Minster itself in the light of what the book had to say, the more clearly I understood the point of Dr. Feilden's title.

The Minster is a building full of wonder—immense and beautiful, with an atmosphere all of its own. Its gleaming loveliness almost takes one's breath away. It is wonderful too, because the work of restoration has brought to light so much of its past history that we did not know before. A walk through the foundations in the undercroft is something else almost to take one's breath away. Then again it is wonderful simply because it is still standing. No-one can read this book without failing to realise that not long ago the Minster was on the brink of disaster. What a debt we owe to those people who undertook and financed the rescue operation!

Nevertheless, it would be rash to assume that all is now well and nothing remains to be done. The Appeal made no provision for stone repair and maintenance; and in these fields years of work still lie ahead. The scaffolding around various parts of the building tells its own tale. Furthermore, there is a sense in which any ancient building is "unpredictable". Mediaeval stonework can do strange things.

So while we are immensely proud of and grateful for all the work which this book describes, we cannot afford to rest content. The future will see no diminution of our responsibilities. Meanwhile we can show our pride and gratitude by using the Minster to the full—both in the worship which we offer to God and the service which we offer to our fellow-men.

Ronald Jasper.

FOREWORD

YORK MINSTER is the symbol of the North, the pride of Yorkshire and part of England's national heritage. The farmers from miles around look up from their fields and see the three towers which dominate the Vale of York. The townsman sees the Minster from different angles as it reappears behind an everchanging foreground of mediaeval shops and houses. Support for the appeal to save the Minster in May 1967 came from all over Yorkshire and from far beyond it: all the parishes in the diocese have shown their love for their Mother Church and gifts have come from all the other dioceses of the Northern Province.

As a boy of ten, having been bred on a small ranch in the Okanagon Valley in British Columbia, I came back to England for schooling in Bedford and used to stay for holidays with my godmother in a gracious house in York. She, being a citizen of York, was immensely proud of the Minster; and although a good Quaker she used to take me to services. Then we would walk round and look at the stained glass which she knew well and loved. She it was who told me the story of how this precious glass was saved after the Battle of Marston Moor, when the victorious Roundheads came to York but were prevented from smashing the windows by the drawn sword of their own General Fairfax, himself a Yorkshireman.[1] So I came to sense the wonder of York Minster, and fell in love with the building.

The problems which as surveyor of the fabric I met and I trust I have solved, together with the help of an expert team of engineers, archaeologists, art historians, mechanical and electrical engineers, quantity surveyors, building contractors, managers, foremen and skilled labour, have led me to think about the wonder of York Minster. What is it about this building that inspires so much loyalty and love? What is the wonder of York Minster? As the architect privileged to lead the team who worked to save the Minster, I have been forced to think of its significance; why is it there? how came it to be so large? why so magnificent? The following historical introduction will attempt to answer these questions briefly.

1. These windows are a priceless asset, being the largest collection in our national heritage of mediaeval glass. Among the masterpieces are the Five Sisters window of about 1250 and the great East Window painted by John Thornton of Coventry between 1404 and 1407, depicting a series of scenes from the book of Revelation in an area as large as a tennis court.

CHAPTER ONE

HISTORICAL INTRODUCTION

YORK MINSTER is one of England's greatest mediaeval cathedrals and one of the largest Gothic structures in Europe. It is over 500 feet long and 245 feet wide across the transepts with spans of 45 feet width, while its central tower rises to over 200 feet, being the biggest of its kind in England.

After the Roman conquest of the Brigantes, the city of York became the base camp of the IX Legion in A.D.71 ; and there has been continuous occupation of the site ever since. The Minster was built on the site of the legionary fortress over the *Principia*, the headquarters building, which was not only the military headquarters but also the seat of provincial government and, on occasion, of imperial government. Whilst London became the capital of southern Britain and the chief commercial centre, York was the military and administrative headquarters. The Principia was the largest and most impressive building in the whole province of Brittania Inferior (further Britain) : and its main hall, the basilica, was almost as large as the transepts and crossings of the Minster, that is approximately 200 feet x 95 feet. The whole Principia was probably 230 feet x 300 feet in area.

In Roman times the Emperors Hadrian, Septimus Severus, Constantius Chlorus and Constantine the Great all visited York; and it was Constantine who was proclaimed Emperor in York probably from the headquarters building, whose principal doorway lies under the steps to the south transept of the Minster. It was also Constantine who established Christianity as the official religion of the Empire. The archaeological excavations on the site have shown that during the Dark Ages, after the withdrawal of the Roman legions in A.D.410 the Roman buildings continued in use for two or even three centuries and may in fact have been rebuilt.

The legends of King Arthur were in all probability based upon the exploits of several British cavalry leaders, the successors of the departed legions who resisted the sea-borne Saxon pagan invaders from the East. The Saxon Chronicle records that King Arthur wintered in York and celebrated the feast of Christmas for the first time in Britain. It is tempting to presume that, as the headquarters building was standing in all its unquestioned grandeur at that time, the feast must have taken place within the basilica.

The position of the present Minster is traditionally related to the baptism of Edwin, King of Northumbria in A.D.627. For this ceremony an oratory was erected; and if his palace consisted of the Roman commander's house—as would be likely—bearing in mind the continued existence and use of the Roman buildings, then archaeological evidence and tradition accord well; as the eastern crypt of the Minster under the high altar is the reputed site of this event. However, with the major Roman buildings still standing, it was more difficult to find a site for the new church which the first Archbishop of York, St. Paulinus, was in haste to see built: but probably the first cathedral building conformed to Roman alignments, and might well have been built of salvaged Roman stone. Paulinus' church may have been a round-ended Saxon structure similar in dimensions to St. Augustine's in Canterbury, or Brixworth near Northampton which were contemporary.

The first Minster was damaged by fire and had to be repaired or replaced in A.D.780. At that time York had become a great centre of learning with a reputation throughout Europe. It was from York that Charlemagne called Alcuin in A.D.800 to become, in effect, his Minister for Education; and it was Alcuin who set up the schools attached to monasteries to which the present day system of education owes its origins. The University of York has honoured Alcuin by naming one of its colleges after him. Historically and archaeologically we are on firmer ground in the 11th and 12th centuries. Shortly after the Norman Conquest York rebelled against William the Conqueror; and in the tumult much of the City of York and the Minster with Alcuin's incomparable library were burnt in 1069.

The new Archbishop of York, Thomas of Bayeux, made temporary repairs to the Saxon building; but ten years later in A.D.1080 ordered a Norman Romanesque building to be constructed of a type unique in England. This was laid out on a true east-west axis, superimposed at an angle of about 43 degrees over the remains of both Roman and Saxon buildings. There was nothing else like it in England for sheer size and plan form. Few buildings in Europe at that time had clear spans of 45 feet; and it is this remarkable dimension that set the scale for the subsequent rebuilding of the Minster. When aisles were added, the total internal width was approximately 100 feet. There was a central tower some 60 feet square; western towers were added to Thomas' cathedral, and there were major modifications to the east end to meet changes in the liturgy. Of that structure we have today exposed the foundations in part in the undercroft while some fragments of Norman masonry are incorporated in the nave and transept walls near the crossing 50 feet above floor level.

There was a fire in 1187; and Archbishop Roger was forced to repair Thomas' church by rebuilding the choir in 1190. He also raised the floor level of the nave some 5 feet; with the result that when the central tower and nave piers were rebuilt at the end of the 14th century, they stood on Norman work only designed as simple walling never intended to take such vast additional loads. Hence the subsequent cause of fatigue in this section of the fabric.

The present Minster began to emerge during the long archbishopric of Walter de Grey, Chancellor to Henry III. The dimensions of the transepts were set by Thomas' work, but aisles were added on the east and west. The central crossing was marked by an early English campanile, incorporating much of Thomas' central tower. Indications of this campanile are given on an ancient seal in the Minster library. After completion of the transepts the remarkable chapter house and vestibule were built in the second half of the 13th century. The chapter house is assumed to have had a stone vault which is believed to have collapsed after some twenty years; the vault design was then altered from stone to a clear span of timber. This structure is of remarkable design, which can be seen in a model displayed in the Minster; and it is one of the great triumphs of English mediaeval carpentry. The presumed collapse was due to the nature of the soil beneath the building; and the reader will come to realise that this was the first piece of historic evidence relating to the problems faced in the recently completed restoration work. The master masons of the Minster reacted to this event by wisely not building stone vaults in the transepts, nave and choir. It should be noted that the vaults were generally built after the roof was covered in; and sometimes as much as forty or fifty years would elapse, as in the case of the nave.

The nave was built between 1303 and 1333. Many of the stained glass windows date from that time; and along with them about 25 panels of glass from the choir of the 12th century cathedral were incorporated into the clerestory. At the east end the late Norman choir was extended by four bays starting in 1361 to form the lady chapel, in which the great Alpha and Omega window by John Thornton of Coventry was completed in 1407. Then the choir was rebuilt, utilising Norman material to recreate the eastern crypt, the Zouche chapel and the vestries.

Then came the work of rebuilding the central tower, which at that time consisted of a 13th century campanile or bell tower. The core of the main piers was 11th century Norman work as were the foundations, over which a layer of 13th century masonry had been applied. The work of altering this to the present design was carried out by removing the 13th century facing and adding a new casing of fine jointed stone. Work must have been well advanced, when in 1406 there was a major collapse in the south westerly direction. Henry IV sent his own master mason, William of Colchester, to supervise the repairs until 1420. The settlement preceding collapse had also caused distortions to the arcades in both north and south transepts, which remain to the present day.

In the last quarter of the century the upper parts of the western towers were built and the choir screen added. The whole Minster was in effect complete by 1472-the work of about ten or twelve master masons over 250 years.

For so many individuals over such a long period to have produced a masterpiece so unified in concept and scale is evidence of the respect the Gothic mason held for the work of his predecessors.

In 1730 William Kent and Lord Burlington repaved the building, raising the level about twelve inches above its previous floor, and strengthened the abutments of the central tower by filling in the first bays of the transept arcades with solid masonry. Then two grievous fires followed. One in 1829 destroyed the choir with its mediaeval stalls and carved work; the roof was rebuilt in teak and the restoration carried out by Sir Sidney Smirke. The second was in 1840, this time in the nave and the south aisle; the repairs were carried out by Sir Sidney's brother Robert. In the late 1860's Edmund Street restored and "improved" the south transept, and between 1890 and 1910 G. F. Bodley added the pinnacles and flying buttresses to the nave.

CHAPTER TWO

THE APPEAL FOR TWO MILLION POUNDS

WHEN the Dean and Chapter appointed me surveyor of York Minster in June 1965, they made it clear that they wanted an architect with some knowledge of Gothic construction as well as one able to deal with all the complex matters of taste and propriety which are so relevant to the design of projects in cathedrals. I felt very honoured by this appointment and realised that I was treading in the steps of such eminent men as Carr of York, G. E. Street and G. F. Bodley as well as my predecessor and teacher, Sir Albert Richardson, P.R.A.

Following my appointment I was instructed to make a detailed inspection of the whole fabric. It is easy to lose one's way in the maze of detail in a Gothic building, for the discipline of inspecting a fabric such as that of York Minster is demanding. First one has to describe and analyse the building; then one has to inspect it part by part, and one's work must be intelligible to subsequent surveyors and be a basis for further inspections. To do this I made a standard approach to each bay which corresponded to the repetition of the Gothic design. It took two years and about 2,000 man hours to inspect the Minster for the first time stone by stone. I had no preconceived ideas; but from a preliminary walk round it was obvious that the east end was leaning out and that there were severe distortions in the transepts adjoining the central tower.

About half way through the inspection I came on fresh cracks in the piers of the central tower and noticed further cracks in the piers of the choir. I advised the Dean and Chapter that a second opinion should be sought from a consulting engineer and recommended that Mr. Geoffrey Wood of Ove Arup & Partners should be instructed. He proposed that some excavation should be carried out close to the north-east pier to show the condition of the foundations. One cannot simply dig a hole in the middle of York Minster without questions being asked; and it was decided that, as there might be a possibility of finding traces of the wooden structure of Edwin's Oratory or one of the early Saxon churches on the site of the Minster, an archaeologist experienced in this field should be asked to carry out the excavation.

Dr. Brian Hope-Taylor of the Cambridge School of Archaeology was accordingly asked to come and carry out the excavation, in which he was assisted by the Minster masons. He gave weekly progress reports, showed people what he was doing and managed skilfully to conceal the rather obvious cracks from too inquisitive eyes by putting tapes or ladders over them. Glass telltales were fixed to various cracks and these were kept under observation. From my inspection it was also clear that a considerable amount of repairs to the stone of the Minster and the roofs would be necessary, besides the major works which would be required to stabilise the east end, the central tower and the western towers.

The Dean and the Canon-Treasurer were particularly concerned about the problems in front of them; and I remember the Dean looking at the hole which Dr. Brian Hope-Taylor had opened up and asking me what could be done if we had to strengthen the foundations of the central tower. I was somewhat daunted by the size of this problem but replied that all I could think of doing was clamping on some large blocks of concrete to the existing foundations in order to increase their load bearing area. However, in the event it was not as simple as that, as we had no knowledge of the subsoil and its load bearing capacity.

In January 1967 Geoffrey Wood and I presented our report to the Greater Chapter. We explained that major works would be necessary to the foundations of the central tower, the east end, the western towers and possibly the choir and nave piers; and it was agreed that an appeal would be necessary.

We stressed that we were concerned not so much with the immediate collapse of the central tower, but with the capability of the structure to withstand the necessary surgery. The problem of the east end could be met by putting up shoring. But for the central tower shoring would be impossible: and this gave the work an additional urgency.

The Earl of Scarbrough, who had been appointed the first High Steward of the Minster, asked to see me and wished to be shown the evidence of what was causing so much concern. I suggested that he should put on overalls and a helmet, and then we should climb up into the choir triforium in order to look at various cracks and pressure points. He gallantly climbed some sixty feet up circular staircases and along galleries without much handrailing, and came to the south-east abutment of the central tower. Here diagonal cracks gave evidence of complex troubles; further cracks in each bay reinforced the story of structural movements. When Lord Scarbrough had seen enough, we returned to the Deanery; and after getting clean from this dirty expedition, and while waiting for a cup of tea, Lord Scarbrough turned to me and said, 'What would it cost to restore the Minster?' I replied that it was difficult to give a firm estimate because there were so many doubtful factors, but that I thought it would cost between £1.67 and £2.5 million pounds. He looked me in the eye for what seemed like a minute and then simply said, 'It can be done'. From that moment he set about leading the appeal and organising the massive support which enabled the work of saving the Minster to be carried out as fast as possible.

After discussion with the Dean and Chapter, Lord Scarbrough decided to launch the appeal in May 1967. This put great pressure on myself and all the other professional advisers, as we had so much work to do. It was recognised that we had only just begun the full detailed investigation of York Minster. The visual inspection had given a general purpose and had indicated the sensitive areas which would require attention. It was clear that an intricate and complicated job had to be carried out, and a team had to be organised which would see it through. As an immediate safety precaution it was decided to strap up the four main piers of the central tower and the piers of the choir where these were cracked. In this phase it was very difficult to maintain security about our intentions, and the story of York Minster Appeal might have leaked to the press. Lord Scarbrough therefore addressed the editors of the various northern newspapers at a luncheon in the Mansion House and explained the position to them. One enterprising young reporter discovered the whole story; but I imagine his editor kept to the agreement reached with Lord Scarbrough. It was decided to hold a press conference in April as a prelude to the launching of the appeal in May. My office assisted me in preparing schematic diagrams to show what had to be done to the Minster.

We consulted the City Engineer and Building Inspector, who helped us with all the information they had about foundations in York. This information, however, was utterly discouraging; and at that time the only possible solution seemed to be the provision of piles arranged so as to support the central tower. Messrs. Arup and I agreed that the central tower was the most urgent problem because it was of a greater dimension than anything we had met. Its peculiar difficulty was that if anything did go wrong, there was no temporary way of supporting it, because sufficient foundation area was simply not available.

To double-check the work of my inspection and make its results readily comprehensible, my office prepared a perspex model of the Minster on which every crack was shown. This was of great assistance, as internal and external cracks could be correlated and the general syndrome of cracking studied. It should be emphasised here and now that not all cracks are bad. In fact, many cracks are necessary to allow the building to expand and contract by day and by night and in accordance with the seasons. The model did show, however, a great concentration of cracks in the abutments of the main piers of the central tower, in the walls adjoining the east end and in the western towers. It is curious to think that if one had cracks $1\frac{1}{4}$ inches wide in a modern block of flats 200 feet high through which wind and rain penetrated, that immediate action would be taken. However, because the Minster is inaccessible and it is difficult to see all these things, this situation had not been previously commented upon. However, the most significant evidence was not in the largest cracks, but in the new cracks in the piers of the central tower and eastern crypt. Here, one of the glass telltales in the south-east pier cracked in February, and this was followed shortly afterwards by two further telltales in the foundations of the north-east pier. This movement in the foundations was particularly significant.

Although I had the best engineering advice obtainable, I suggested that I should get a further opinion from another cathedral architect. Just as in matters of life and death surgeons seek consultation, so in deciding upon the need for repairs to a national monument and the method of treating them, a second opinion was highly desirable. Mr. Robert Potter, who for ten years had been dealing with similar problems in Chichester Cathedral, was invited to come and make a report. His report read as follows:

> "I have been requested by Mr. Bernard Feilden to examine his recent report upon the fabric of York Minster and to offer comments in the form of a second opinion, and this I now have the honour of presenting to you.
>
> Mr. Feilden's report represents a very thorough and painstaking documentation of the present condition of the building and provides a valuable record not only for present analysis and action but also as a basis for future observations. In the limited time at my disposal I have concentrated upon the more serious aspects of structural weaknesses and in particular those affecting the central tower and its abutments. At my inspection of the Minster I was impressed by the widespread pattern of settlements which extend throughout the arcades and by the appreciable disturbance in the masonry, both at the abutments to the central tower and in the structure of the lantern. The architectural pattern and scale of the present Minster which evolved from the building of the south transept in the 13th century and which set the module for the nave and the rebuilding of the eastern arm is direct and uncomplicated; the materials and craftsmanship are of the finest.
>
> Had the foundations rested upon a compact gravel as at Salisbury, I am confident that there would have been no cause for concern for its behaviour today, even after the addition of the tall lantern. I think it is of importance to note that the central

spaces were completed with wooden vaults indicating without doubt that the master masons were apprehensive of the behaviour of the foundations and of the potential danger in poising heavy masonry vaults upon the arcades. Without the evidence of a detailed soil analysis extending to an appreciable depth, I would not be prepared to comment upon the bearing capacity of the subsoil. Suffice it to say, however, that the nature of the settlements in the fabric demonstrate that it has proved inadequate to support in a level plane the present structure, with the result that uneven settlement has tended to separate the structural elements in the planes of greatest weakness; this is true both in the arcades of nave, choir and transepts as it is throughout the height of the tower itself.

The pattern of settlements in the tower indicate an outward movement of the walls at parapet level, the masonry spandrels over the great arches have sheared on the oblique line of thrust and in the transepts horizontal movement outwards has occurred at the abutments-this is particularly noticeable in the arcading of the south transept. There is a natural tendency for massive gable walls to rotate outwards and this tendency undoubtedly occurred in the south transept prior to the major restoration and reinforcement of this transept by Street. The appreciable extent to which the lantern and its supporting piers have settled is evidenced at the abutments, triforium and clerestory level-a sinkage of more than six inches. The total settlement in the foundations cannot, of course, be estimated but evidence of shearing has been revealed and is illustrated in the photographs taken of the excavations at the base of the north east pier and can also be seen in the walling supporting the choir piers at crypt level.

It has taken several centuries for the movement within the structure to develop to its present stage, and from a visual inspection of some of the settlements it would appear certain that this movement is continuing. It is of importance, however, to be able to measure with accuracy the extent and direction of this movement to enable the cause to be more accurately determined. My first recommendation is that a pattern of telltales of the 3-pin type should be set up throughout the Minster and throughout the full height of the tower and its abutments in particular. Measurements should be taken and recorded at regular intervals, not less than quarterly. In addition, it would be helpful if a date and level could be established on each pier to the central tower and its level related to a specially driven pile sunk in some suitable position well clear of the external walls of the building from which to obtain levels and observations of any further sinking of the great piers.

The stresses in the masonry, particularly in the piers, have undoubtedly been affected over the centuries by the dehydration and weakening of the lime mortar infilling, a process which was undoubtedly accelerated where the masonry was subjected to the fires of 1829 and 1840 which severely damaged the nave and choir respectively. As a result of this it must be assumed that the weight of the structure should not be considered to be carried on the masonry skins which are probably nor more than 12 inches in thickness, if that. From my own approximate calculation and taking into account the degree of eccentricity in the loading of the piers, I would estimate that the factor of safety from the crushing of the stone has been reduced in the order of 11 to 3. The failures that have occurred are not, in fact, due to crushing but to shear arising from the process of articulation due to movements in the foundations.

The excavations at the base of the north east pier reveal that the 15th century casing which rise above the present floor level which were executed under the direction of William Colechester following the fall of the belfry rest upon the work of at least two successive periods. At the lowest level exposed to a depth of approximately 10 feet below that of the nave, the stones were found to be embedded in a mortar of good quality and containing ash, an ingredient to improve the setting of the lime following the Roman and early Saxon practice of the use of ground tile for this purpose. It was interesting to discover Roman tile creasing used in the northern arm for the reinforcement of the masonry. I would suggest that this work dates from and forms part of the third Minster of Archbishop Thomas and the apsidal eastern end of the church discovered in the crypt.

The masonry above this level is constructed in a mortar of poor quality with very little lime and free of ash. The quality of building of the central tower was of this standard-here lies a good reason for its collapse.

The 15th century masonry, however, is work of the highest quality and is embedded in a rich lime mortar made with a very fine sand. It cannot be certain whether the piers were largely rebuilt or merely encased by William Colechester-it would be safer, however, to assume the latter. The manner in which the piers rest upon the ancient foundations, however, gives reason for the severe shear stresses which have occurred in the piers. Further evidence is required in the form of accurate plumbing throughout the height of the tower at each angle to determine more precisely the extent of lateral movement in the upper parts of the building.

The full depth of the foundation had not been probed at the time of my visit and I think it is important to discover whether the foundations of the building reach to the Roman pavement level or whether indeed they rest on made ground. The levels of the timber rafts as indicated in Mr. Feilden's drawing would suggest that the 11th century building and its 12th century successor may well have been so founded and this could account, or at least give a good reason, for the second rebuilding of the choir.

From the foregoing I am in no doubt as to the cause of the behaviour of the building which can be attributed either directly or indirectly to its foundations. In the absence of an accurate record of movement in the structure, I am unable to predict the period, when a continuance of the present movement will lead to eventual collapse. I am however, convinced that the stage has been reached when effective measures should be taken to reinforce and integrate the structure to prevent its collapse and substantially improve the bearing ability of the foundations to the piers of the central and western towers. It is quite impracticable to think in terms of underpinning the whole of the foundations; the approach, I believe, should be to tune such movement as will inevitably occur within limits which will reduce uneven settlement. The reinforcement of the structure must take into account a degree of flexibility in some of its connections, e.g. the central tower should be—so far as it is practicable—considered as a separate structural entity secured within itself and without reliance on the counter thrusts from the arcades and free to move in a vertical plane without damage to the remainder of the building. Such measures are practicable but they will need to be worked out with the utmost consideration; and for this reason I would prefer not to comment upon Mr. Feilden's proposals in detail at this stage, but if desired confer further with him on this very important matter.

In principle, however, I have in mind the introduction of a reinforced concrete ring beam at parapet level to prevent the outward spread of the top of the lantern and the introduction of further reinforcement in the form of a corset to secure the spandrels over the great arches and negative lateral thrust and thereby reducing the eccentric loading of the great piers.

In view of the weakness which must be anticipated within the cores of the great piers, it is essential that these should be strengthened; and I am not altogether happy with Mr. Feilden's tentative proposals for this. It is a matter which will need the most careful consideration, having regard to the enormous loads borne by the piers.

The reinforcement of the foundations calls for a specialised knowledge of soil mechanics and I understand that Messrs. Ove Arup have been appointed consulting engineers to advise on this important problem. It is of the utmost importance that the engineer and the architect should work together as a team to share and benefit from their specialist experiences. Reference has been made to the possible effect of recent changes in the water table. Such changes must have occurred when the tidal part of the Ouse was regulated in the 18th century. The lowering of the water-table—if this has, in fact, recently occurred—might well accelerate the compaction of the subsoil increasing at least for a time the rate of movement within the building; it could certainly worsen the present situation.

Considerable thought needs to be given to the programme for repair and reinforcement. I would agree that the securing of the tower piers and lantern should receive first consideration; but if this is likely to involve an appreciable addition to the weight of the structure, then it may be found preferable to provide temporary cradling and perimeter ties to the lantern and to proceed with the reinforcement of the foundations of the great piers as a first priority.

It will obviously be impracticable totally to underpin the foundations of the piers but

I am confident that a containing reinforced concrete girdle resting upon a system of Pali Ridicci piles[1] could be designed by the engineers which would have the desired effect. I should be very interested to take part in these consultations if so desired.

When the necessary action has been completed in the securing of the central tower and its abutments, attention should next be directed in a similar manner to the two western towers and this may well involve the reinforcement of the foundations of the western piers and of the structure at high level. Measurements from the 3-pin tell-tales will indicate the extent of any further movement in the meanwhile and ample warning should be available should it become necessary to prevent the ringing of the bells. In this respect I would suggest that the bell tower be inspected by Mr. Ranold Clouston and seismograph readings taken indicating the extent of gyration at bell cage level.

I have but cursorily examined the general condition of the external masonry, but it is evident that a substantial programme of masonry repairs exists and in the light of experience I would say that a programmed expenditure of £30,000 to £35,000 per year is indeed a modest estimate, having regard to the backlog which must be overtaken.

In conclusion, I would most strongly support an appeal to undertake immediately the structural needs of the cathedral and a programme for its general repair and conservation.

A press conference was held on April 7th, and I was asked to explain the problems of the Minster. This was an ordeal; but fortified by the support of Geoffrey Wood and Robert Potter I felt confident that we had analysed the problems of the Minster correctly, and that we could find a solution to the problems. The Dean and Chapter thoroughly supported, and may I say, blessed our efforts.

At a receptive meeting in the Guildhall on May 11th 1967, over which the Lord Mayor of York presided, the appeal was launched with a target of £2 million. It was a wonderful experience hearing the speeches from miners, farmers, citizens of York, academics and churchmen stating what York Minster meant to them. The depth of their feeling, love and affection for the Minster was truly remarkable; and on an occasion such as this, one could feel the strong pulse of Yorkshiremen and their pride and determination to see that the Minster should not suffer any disaster. The sight of the foundations and the condition of the masonry had convinced me that the Minster was in a critical condition, and when pressed I gave the central tower a life of some fifteen years. More telltales broke, and early in July six broke in one week. The total score was then sixteen.

By then glass telltales had been superseded by more accurate Demec Gauge measurements, which showed active movements in the central tower foundations. Here the way the telltales broke also suggested that the piers were driving down through the weak masonry of the Norman foundations in such a way as to burst them apart.

1. Pali Ridicci are piles of 6 or 9 inches diameter drilled at an angle to the vertical so as to spread loads over a wide area. They were one of the proprietary systems which were examined.

CHAPTER THREE

INVESTIGATION AND EXCAVATION

MESSRS. SHEPHERD were appointed to carry out the works; and from the very beginning the consulting engineers and all advisers had the best and most friendly formal and informal relations. This helped the work on the Minster immensely. In true teamwork you do not expect everyone to agree all the time, but you do expect the best solution to evolve; and in a job as large and complex as the Minster, every man had his part to play. Where differences of opinion existed they were held honestly and were resolved creatively for the benefit of the Minster. We all put the Minster first and became her servants.

A full site investigation was commissioned under the direction of Messrs. Arup with Messrs. Marples Ridgeway Limited. Bore holes were dug, and soil sample cores were taken and analysed. All core holes were plugged with concrete as a precaution against altering the watertable. A datum is a fixed immovable point of reference for survey work. As the Minster itself was moving and soil is compressible it was necessary to drill to the solid rock some 80 feet below to get a satisfactory datum. Two deep datum points were inserted, one inside the Minster and one outside.

In the meantime, cores were taken from the main piers and choir piers in order to see how they were constructed. The choir piers were of good ashlar masonry throughout their thickness but had been partially refaced following the 1829 fire. The cores showed that the cracks were due to shrinkages in the freshly quarried stone of the repairs following that fire. The central piers were much more complicated, the core being a mixture of rubble masonry and brown mortar, the middle part consisting of rubble masonry and white mortar, and the visible outer casing of fine jointed ashlar blocks. It is probable that the brown mortar was Norman, the white mortar early English and the outer casing as we all know dating from the reconstruction of the central tower in 1406-1450. The ratio of the stone and mortar varied from 30% to 70% with 30%-70% stone in the core, whilst the outside casing was about 98% stone and 2% mortar. Built in three periods and of such varying material, it was difficult to imagine the pier acting homogeneously.

It is probable that each pier was built at four slightly separated dates as there are straight joints. Unfortunately there was so much dirt on the masonry that it was hard to make a detailed inspection; but in due course it was hoped to resolve the problem of the sequence of building of the piers of the central tower. However, at that stage we were totally unaware of several important factors in the history of the Minster. These only emerged as a result of the archaeological excavations, which have thrown much light on the problems of the Minster and have assisted the engineers and myself in assessing the structural requirements. The soil mechanics cores did reveal certain surprising things. First, some Roman masonry was found at the great depth of 25 feet close to the north-west pier, probably from a Roman well under the main foundations. Then the bore hole between the south choir aisle and lady chapel also showed a layer of burnt ash at a depth of about 12 feet. Even having the past histories and accounts of the Minster, it must be stated that at that stage our knowledge was very incomplete. Thinking that I knew a little about Norman towers, having had the care of the finest one in the country for some ten years[1], I found it difficult to imagine York Minster having a 60 foot square tower dating from the 11th century. I was also puzzled and intrigued by the sheer size of the Minster, and I asked myself, "How did it come to be built so big?" and "Why was such size necessary?" These questions are now of course answered by the archaeological excavation.

During the site investigations I had many discussions with the consulting engineers, each of us modifying the other in his approach to the problem. We agreed that the principal difficulty of carrying out the work of restoration lay in technique. Technique or contracting 'know-how' is the province of contractors, and we therefore consulted four firms and asked them for their proposals. Messrs. Cementation produced a solution very similar to that which we finally adopted, and very similar to what I had first suggested to the Dean. They proposed piles with large pile caps attached to the Norman masonry. Messrs. Pinford proposed underpinning the central piers using steel stools to insert a large footing under each pier. Messrs. Forakay suggested freezing the ground in order to excavate a vertical shaft under each pier and insert a caisson, or vertical shaft of concrete some 10 feet in diameter to carry the load of the piers down to the rock below. Lastly, Messrs. Fondedile suggested drilling 40 radial piles at an acute angle through each pier down into underlying sandstone. Every proposal was carefully weighed and the pros and cons discussed by Messrs. Arup and myself. There were two fundamental problems to solve. First, how to increase the load bearing area of the main piers, at the same time reducing the eccentric loading on the foundations; and secondly, how to contain the existing fatigued masonry in such a way that it would not burst. At the same time it was realised that the structure would not stand much disturbance as the masonry was much fatigued. The principles of conservative repair should be observed, in that maximum use should be made of existing structural material.

The results of the soil investigation came in a massive report; and when these were assessed we realised that we were more fortunate than we had expected, for only three or four feet below the existing Norman masonry lay a good stratum of clay. Also, contrary to local knowledge, which indicated that we should expect glacial rubbish and very mixed strata, we found regular and even strata under the whole of the Minster site. The idea of piled foundations could be abandoned and it was possible to design enlarged footings to take the weight of the central tower, retaining the existing masonry but encasing it completely in new reinforced concrete.

Using the perspex model, Robert Potter and I had made an initial analysis of the structural movements in the Minster. This was now later confirmed by Arup's computer analysis, which in addition quantified all the forces and lines of thrust in the central tower. It was found that the loads on the central tower piers were very eccentric; and the loading on the worst side was of the order of 8 tons per square foot. This figure coincided with what we had found to be the ultimate stress of the clay at this level, giving scientific confirmation to the results of my visual inspection. Clearly the situation with regard to the foundations was critical, and there was also a danger of uplift in the adjacent areas, by the soil under the foundations being squeezed outwards. It is not generally realised that the soil on which most buildings rest is semi-fluid and capable of

1. The central tower of Norwich Cathedral built c.1130.

moving to quite a remarkable degree. It is even said that the Tower of London moves up and down slightly with the tides in the Thames.

Careful measurement of the structure and comparison of levels carried out by David Dowrick revealed that the north-west pier of the central tower had settled some 12½ inches and the other piers some 8½ inches. The consulting engineers were persuaded to make a study of the foundation movements in the Minster since it was built. This was considered necessary and desirable so that the importance of present cracks could be assessed. This study integrated historical knowledge with factual measurements and the science of soil mechanics. Such multi-disciplinary studies are the essence of the conservation of buildings. From this study it was found that the whole nave had settled some 4 inches quite shortly after being constructed and then remained comparatively stable; but that the Norman central tower had settled about 8 inches when further weight had been added during the early English period; for it was discovered that a campanile had been built at the same time as the transepts. The archaeologists had found the remains of this campanile in the foundations, so the early historical documents were re-studied; and it was agreed conclusively that there had been an early English bell tower or campanile. This fact had appeared in none of the previous histories of the Minster. It was further corroborated at a later date when remains of the casting pits for the bells were found by Mr. Herman Ramm in the north transept area.

After a full investigation of the subsoil and further detailed measurements of the movements in the superstructure, Messrs. Arup felt in a position to consider the design of the new foundations themselves. They proposed adding large areas of concrete on three sides of each pier and to include the first pier of the transepts, nave and choir within the general scheme of enlarged footings. They also proposed a collar round the upper part of the foundations. This upper part had originally been walling to support a low Norman tower. It had never been designed to carry a quarter of the 16,000 ton weight of the central tower. The mortar was soft, crumbling and de-natured; but if it were to be totally contained by a casing of reinforced concrete this would not matter. During the design phase the principle of conservation that the best use should be made of existing material was borne in mind. The second rule that conservation work should be invisible if at all possible was also followed. The reinforcement was placed diagonally under each pier so as to pick up the weight more effectively. This would involve longer drilling shots; but the contractor, who by then had some experience of drilling long holes in the middle of the tower, was confident that this could be done. The special feature that Arup introduced was the compression pad with inflatable Fressynet jacks. The idea was that when the drilling and prestressing of the foundations was complete, these hydraulic jacks should be inflated and then they would press a large mass of concrete down into the clay foundations, causing the new foundations to take up their share of the massive load equally with the old foundations without further settlements.

Mr. Potter, together with Mr. T. A. Bailey, then Chief Architect of the Ancient Monuments Department of the Ministry of Public Building and Works, continued in their consultant capacity. It is very useful to have critics who are not involved in the day-to-day running of a project to take a fresh look at what one is doing every six months, and I valued the help and comments of these my colleagues who came at about six-monthly intervals. Mr. Potter had some reservations about the implications of drilling four rows of $1\frac{1}{4}$ inch rods diagonally under the north-west pier as he was afraid that this might induce a collapse. However, it was agreed that all we could do was try and see how it worked. Bearing Mr. Potter's reservations in mind, Messrs. Shepherd were careful to pre-grout the area to be drilled as fully as possible, as this would contribute to the safety of the operation and make accurate drilling more possible; and it was found necessary to sleeve the holes after drilling, thus endorsing Mr. Potter's advice.

Whilst design work was going on in the central tower, it was thought expedient to dig an exploratory trench at the east end. This was done under archaeological direction, and a depth of about 8 feet below street level reached. Poul Beckmann, the associate partner in charge of the Arup Team, and I were in no doubt when we looked into this pit that some urgent action would have to be taken to ensure the stability of the east end, which we knew was leaning outwards some 25 inches. We were particularly concerned, because six telltales had cracked in this area recently. Messrs. Arup did a design study and specified that a horizontal thrust of approximately 20 tons should be applied at a height of 80 feet. Messrs. Pickup of Scarborough and Messrs. Shepherd produced designs for the shoring which were approved by Messrs. Arup; work was put in hand without delay, but there was some anxiety particularly amongst the parents of the children from the school nearby. It was my duty to reassure them that we were keeping a day-to-day check on the movements in this area, and that their children were not at risk; but with memories of Aberfan fresh in everyone's mind this was not an easy task. In designing this shoring a third principle of conservation was brought into play, that new work must not be too strong for the old work. In order to make the shoring kind to the old fabric it was decided to rest the base on four Fressynet jacks which would maintain the correct horizontal pressure constantly; and if thermal or other movements took place these jacks could compensate for this by expanding or contracting. This arrangement proved effective; and the jacks moved about three-quarters of an inch, thereby saving possible damage to the Minster.

We now had two first priority jobs on our hands, the foundations for both the central tower and the east end; but we were also concerned to strengthen and stabilise the superstructure of the central tower and also the north-west tower, which had already been scaffolded in 1966 for the restoration of pinnacles under my predecessor.

An internal scaffold was built inside the central tower and externally the lower part of the tower was ringed with scaffolding. The first major drilling was attempted when inserting a girdle of 12 stainless steel rods in each side of the central tower at mid-height. This drilling had to be surveyed with great accuracy, and when the drills were set up they then nibbled their way through the masonry. It was found that the masonry was fissured, and that the voids were causing the drills to run crookedly, and accordingly the area to be strengthened had to be pre-grouted. The grouting improved matters, but could not replace areas of soft stone or lime mortar, and could not be guaranteed to fill all voids. However, a special hollow tube, the full diameter of the shaft was designed to follow the drill and pass the waste backwards; and with this remarkable accuracy was achieved by the drilling team. These holes 68 feet in length drilled through fissured masonry are a great tribute to Messrs. Shepherd's skill. I well remember the arrival of the first drill through the north face of the tower—it was like the birth of a baby—one listened for the heart beats or the sound of the drill and awaited its arrival. It seemed never to come-then suddenly it was there and everyone was overjoyed. After drilling the holes, threaded stainless steel rods were passed down the holes in 15 foot lengths and jointed with couplers, then finally anchored at each end and stressed lightly with hydraulic jacks. After this stressing they were grouted into position and became fully bonded to the stone. In this way an invisible repair with good adhesion to the masonry was achieved. This girdle has an important strengthening effect on the tower and gave more confidence with regard to the work which was being carried on below.

Following the girdle, the top of the central tower was strengthened. The ends of nearly all the 15th century main beams had been badly attacked and most of the secondary timbers were also riddled with deathwatch beetle. There had been a previous repair in the 19th century, when large cast iron brackets had been attached to the decayed ends of the beams.

Here a ring beam was necessary; and sadly the old 50 feet long 15th century oak beams had to be removed. Their removal created quite a considerable problem as they had to be sawed into small, manageable lengths, then lowered carefully in specially prepared steel containers and carried down the hoist. Mr. Stephens of Messrs. Shepherd arranged so that the light steel frame supporting the roof was made strong enough to lift and hoist the sawn-up oak pieces, so that they could be lowered safely some 200 feet. The small amount of timber that was re-useable was converted into objects for sale in the Minster shop.

When the old roof had been stripped and cleared away, it was possible to cast the new reinforced concrete ring beam which was anchored to the stone by long stainless steel dowels. The casting of this was quite an event as concrete was pumped up 200 feet. By noon of the same day 90 cubic yards had been lifted into position and the job was complete. It took the rest of the day to dismantle and clean the piping up which the concrete had come, but this operation was certainly a tribute to the technical ingenuity and the efficiency of the contractors. It probably would have taken at least three weeks to lift the amount of concrete required by the hoist, carrying a barrow load at a time.[1]

The ring beam was followed by the insertion of six steel beams which supported a wooden roof structure covered by 8 lb. cast lead sheets laid by Messrs. Norman & Underwood. When the external work was completed, the temporary superstructure was removed and a new hatch giving access to the roof provided. The walkways round the roof have been made wider than before and are lined with epoxy resin. The rainwater outlets were doubled to prevent blockages and now have electric tracer cables wound round the pipework where it is embedded in the concrete in order to prevent freezing up and blockage by ice. The tower was re-opened to the public on July 6th, 1970.

1. This achievement was specially commended by Cembureau at the 1975 European Architectural Heritage Year Conference at Amsterdam.

CHAPTER FOUR

ARCHAEOLOGICAL ASPECTS

TO RETURN to the main works, to which the repair of the superstructure of the central tower was entirely secondary, the procedure here was for the overburden down to 6 feet to be removed by Messrs. Shepherd, who arranged an ingenious internal railway system. Then the remainder of the excavation at lower levels was carried out under archaeological supervision—in the first year in charge of Mr. Herman Ramm (who was kindly seconded from the Royal Commission on Historical Monuments). He was then succeeded by Mr. Derek Phillips who had been trained at Durham University under Professor Birley. It was always clear that the excavation was an engineering dig and that the archaeologists were in a secondary capacity. Whenever the programme allowed, however, and something of archaeological importance was found, time was made available for the archaeologists to investigate this point as thoroughly as possible; whilst the contractor employed his men in another area of the excavation. Although not ideal from either party's point of view, this compromise was the best that could be arranged at that time.

The importance of the archaeological information obtained from this excavation cannot yet be assessed, as this will take several years to write up and publish; but "prima facie" it has revealed the Norman plan of the 11th century Minster with subsequent alterations and additions as well as the early English campanile. This plan in itself is quite unique in Britain and answers the question why the Minster was built so large; for Thomas of Bayeux, first Norman Archbishop in 1069, must have stipulated a Rhenish type of Romanesque building with an aisle-less nave of the widest span structurally possible in Britain. This span would in my opinion have been dictated by the length of oak tie beams it was possible to obtain, and this would give a clear span of about 45 feet with a beam in the order of 50 feet length. It is interesting to note that the finest oak beams were obtained by Sir Christopher Wren for St. Paul's from the Welbeck Estate in Nottinghamshire, and it is also possible that the oak beams for York Minster came by water from that area. The Minster of Thomas of Bayeux was built of rough masonry and then plastered both internally and externally; probably with small windows and a tall choir, nave and transepts, it must have been a simple but impressive building. It is interesting to remember that the floor level of its nave was some 6 feet below that of the present Minster. The remains of this Norman Minster are to be found in the north and south transepts, where the fragments of a newel staircase exist some 60 feet above ground and in the cores of the central tower piers. These remains have survived the collapse of the early English campanile and the successive alterations in the Minster.

The archaeological evidence of the Saxon period is somewhat confusing. It is indeed remotely possible that the foundations of a large Saxon church remain incorporated within the Norman church between the western piers and the apse, which was marked out in the eastern crypt. Some explanation must be found for the excessive width of these foundations, but this information is not yet forthcoming. The evidence of Saxon graves all set out on the Roman alignment has to be weighed up carefully. Does this alignment of graves conform to the dominating pattern of upstanding remains of Roman buildings, or does it conform to a Saxon church on the Roman alignment? One must await the expert analysis of the evidence by the archaeologists before an opinion can be reached. Nevertheless there is evidence of continuous occupation of the impressive Roman remains throughout the Dark Ages; and this is an immensely significant fact, altering the popular conception of what happened in this period. Many displaced stones of proven Saxon origin have been found; but so far no trace of Edwin's Oratory set up in A.D.627 nor of the subsequent buildings of the 7th and late 8th centuries have been found. It can be said, however, that we know where these buildings are not to be found.

By way of contrast, plentiful Roman remains have been uncovered and these indicate the magnificence of the legionary fortress as established in the 2nd century and how this was subsequently altered. The basilica itself, which lies under the nave and the south transept, was a fine building with columns over 25 feet high, covering an area as large as the nave of the Minster itself. It was one of the largest Roman buildings in Britain.

With so many hazards and unknowns which could affect the detailed design and execution of the work, it was deemed necessary to excavate completely before design could be finally decided. This left an awkward interim period when uplift might occur in the soil carrying the foundation loads owing to the great pressures exerted by the central tower on the ground supporting it. To prevent this uplift, heavy sandbagging was always kept in position round each pier and only one quarter area could be worked on at a time. Time was to prove that this sandbagging was a highly necessary precaution. The second precaution was in the heavy steel strutting which prevented any horizontal bursting action taking place in the foundation masonry. Further excavation had provided more visual evidence that this action was incipient; but when totally encased in concrete the danger was removed. The horizontal strutting was also designed to carry temporary flooring at main church floor level over the whole area.

Many pieces of Roman masonry were uncovered during the excavation, and where possible these were left in situ and the reinforced concrete arranged sympathetically around them. One tall column was removed from under the south transept, and this was later erected by the York Civic Trust on the south side of the Minster to commemorate the 1900th anniversary of the Roman founding of York in A.D.71. Roman works have had some effect on the stability of the Minster. It was found that a Roman water course had run under the north-west pier and that a Roman well was also under this pier; that some Roman walling was incorporated in the foundations of the south-east pier; and that as a result of the settlements the area of this foundation had been greatly reduced by steeply inclined sheer cracks. As a quick guide to the levels in the Minster, Roman works lie at about 12 feet below existing floor level, Saxon about 9 feet to 7 feet, early Norman about 6 feet, late Norman about a foot and a half, early English about one foot three inches, Perpendicular about one foot down. The present floor was laid in the 18th century by William Kent and Lord Burlington with a black key pattern.

This raising of the floor level after the early English building of the south transept left the de Grey Tomb somewhat sunk in the floor; and perhaps here a slight digression on the restoration of the de Grey Tomb would be permissible, for before the results of my inspection could be anticipated a decision to restore this monument had been taken by the Dean and Chapter.

The Dean had, at Lord Stamford's suggestion, arranged a private appeal to raise funds for the restoration of this famous tomb of a much loved Archbishop, who was Edward I's Chancellor for many years and died in 1255. Her Majesty the Queen Mother and the Emperor Haile Selassie had given generously towards this appeal, members of the de Grey Family subscribed, and the Pilgrim Trust very kindly made up the balance after the work had been completed.

The de Grey Tomb restoration had many of the problems of the restoration of the Minster in miniature. Its foundations had failed; and it was tilting 3 inches downwards at the east end and was strutted from the railings that had been put round it in 1804. These railings were interesting examples of early cast iron work but obscured the monument. It was decided to take the monument down piece by piece. Then the effigy had to be lifted; and whilst this was being done the mason noticed a fragment of colour coming out as he carefully sawed through an old lime mortar joint. He stopped and reported this phenomenon. Then under the supervision of Dr. Gee of the Royal Commission on Historical Monuments the slab was lifted and it was found that there was a painted cover on the coffin lid. This is a unique object in England and I am told only one other such painted lid exists in Europe. It was agreed that it should not be covered up but be displayed. But the question was—how? and where?

A conference of all interested parties was held in the chapter house and three alternatives were discussed-

1. To sink the coffin and lid so that it could be viewed through a slit in the floor.

2. To raise the whole monument and leave the present coffin intact and visible.

3. To put the monument in a new position.

There were strong objections to all these courses; and accordingly it was decided that the coffin lid should be lifted and replaced, and the superstructure reinstated in its original position. Arrangements were made so that every expert who might have something to contribute to the success of the operation could be present. However, we forgot that there would also be an interest in the pathological aspects of the interred body.

In the presence of the Dean and Chapter, of the Earl of Stamford, who as head of the de Grey Family had been primarily responsible for the decision to restore this famous monument, and all the experts, the coffin lid was lifted as follows.

About 7.30 p.m. on May 3rd, 1968, the Dean and Chapter with the Bishop of Selby as the Archbishop's representative and Lord Stamford assembled together with Brigadier Hadden, the Chapter Clerk. The late Canon Purvis was present together with Sir Mortimer Wheeler, Dr. Ralegh Radford and Mr. Dufty of the Royal Commission on Historical Monuments and his colleagues Dr. Gee, Mr. Ramm, Mr. Harvey, and Mr. Bassham, and Mr. Phillips who was in charge of the archaeological work in the Minster. Experts in conservation had been asked to attend, and Dr. Werner of the British Museum Laboratories came to attend to metal objects, Mr. King and his wife and Mr. Blair came from the Victoria and Albert Museum to look after textiles, and Mr.

Clive Rouse and his assistant Miss Ballantyne were there to attend to the famous painted lid. The stone lid had already been freed from the coffin by sawing through the mortar joint, and nylon slings had been slipped into the crack. There was a scaffold gantry frame above to house the Royal Commission photographer and his lights. The Dean gave his permission, and the Surveyor of the Fabric asked the Superintendent of Works to instruct the Minster masons to lift the lid. It seemed to float upwards guided by Mr. Holland the foreman mason.

There was reverence as all present gazed in silence at the mortal remains of Archbishop de Grey, brilliantly illuminated for the photographer. Then quickly the contents of the tomb were examined. The crozier, chalice and paten were obvious, remains of his leather shoes and a cushion under his head were visible, and after some searching his ring was discovered. This was seen to contain a large jewel and to be set with precious stones, and was obviously of great value and fascinating design.

After a conference the Dean and Chapter, with the approval of Lord Stamford and the Bishop of Selby, decided that it was right and proper to remove the valuable objects from the tomb. Miss Ballantyne deftly cleaned the coffin; then the painted lid was removed to the Minster workshops for treatment under the direction of Mr. Clive Rouse. Next day the textiles were carefully packed for treatment by Mr. King. Dr. M. Barnet and Dr. G. Summers made an anatomical study of the Archbishop's skeleton and took photographs. The Archbishop had died in his seventies and was known to have led a vigorous life. His skeleton was in excellent condition and showed no indication of any serious illness, but there had been an abscess in his teeth in early life.

When all work had been completed, a new Portland stone cover was placed on the coffin and set in mortar. The significance of the objects found in the Archbishop's coffin has been described in *Archaeologia*, Volume CIII by Herman Ramm and others.[1]

On the opening of the coffin I myself was impressed by the dignity of the dead Archbishop who must have been a truly great man. The value of the ring, chalice, paten, crozier and other items far exceeded anything that had been expected, and clearly there was a security problem if these were to be left in the tomb. These objects are now on display in the Minster Undercoft.

1. *The Tombs of Archbishop Walter de Grey (1216-55) and Godfrey de Ludham (1258-65) in York Minster and their contents*, by H. G. Ramm, MA, FSA, et al. Printed by Vivian Ridler for the Society of Antiquaries of London, Oxford 1971.

CHAPTER FIVE

THE EAST END

RETURNING to the east end, while the shoring was being put up, Messrs. Arup were designing the new foundations in consultation with Messrs. Shepherd. It was decided that a large scale underpinning operation should be undertaken, and short tunnels were driven through the old and defective masonry, which was removed in 4 feet wide sections to a careful programme and replaced by a new concrete block some 4 feet wide and 18 feet long from east to west and 9 feet deep. A whole series of these blocks was inserted in agreed order, working first to support the major weights under the piers and buttresses, then at the corners, and finally towards the centre and extremities of the east end. The total foundation was 125 feet long, 18 feet wide and 9 feet deep. The operation went successfully, but as with all underpinning operations there must be some attendant settlement. This settlement accentuated some of the existing cracks between the east wall itself and the north and south side walls, particularly in St. Stephen's Chapel and All Saints' Chapel. Due to the glacial build up of the clay subsoil these movements took place quicker than was expected and a small amount of glass in All Saints' Chapel was cracked. All mediaeval glass was therefore loosened in the north and south walls in the vicinity before further movement took place. However, the main problem of protection of the east window was successfully achieved, and as far as can be told, no differential movement took place in the plane of the east wall. The glass was inspected at weekly intervals. During the foundation operation it was possible to make a close inspection of the tracery in the east window from scaffolding both inside and outside, and it was found that this was bowing out 9 inches more than the east wall-which itself had bowed out 25 inches. After an immense amount of thought and consultation it was agreed that three bow-string ties would strengthen the window and prevent a collapse of the tracery due to wind action. These bow-string ties are like a horizontal suspension bridge with 1 inch stainless steel wires anchored in the side walls and fixed to node points in the tracery. They were tensioned so as to pull the tracery back. As they are visible they can only be considered a semi-permanent repair; and perhaps my successors will be able to find the perfect solution to this problem: but short of taking the glass out and rebuilding the tracery which would be prohibitively expensive, we did our best. These have been put in, and it is hoped that they are not too noticeable. We do not count this as a permanent restoration, because it does not obey the rule that conservation work should be invisible. However, no other viable alternative could be found. The important thing was to prevent a sudden collapse of the east window tracery together with William Thornton's priceless Alpha and Omega window.

Wherever works were carried out on the Minster, it was the policy to make maximum use of the scaffolding for incidental repairs. As various works were finished, the Minster was therefore cleaned down and the stone-work washed. This had an inspiring aesthetic effect; but there was also a sound structural policy behind the cleaning, in that it was necessary to see all the defects and test each individual stone before the work could be said to be complete. Any necessary repairs were carried out by the Minster masons. During the restoration we had several minor falls of stone, and any of these could have been lethal in normal circumstances. As stone is an unpredictable material when in tension, it was only an elementary precaution to test each boss and rib to see that it was firm; and it was found necessary to do a certain amount of repair and reinstatement in both St. Stephen's Chapel, where a boss had fallen, and in All Saints' Chapel where the ribs and brick vaulting and plaster had become loose. The Minster masons were responsible for all stone repairs.

It should also be mentioned that the Minster masons 'heavy gang' under Lew Littlewood had cleaned the chapter house and the chapter house passage in 1969. In the passage it was found that ribs were loose and potentially dangerous. Repairs were authorised by the trustees; and the friable vaulting which was badly cracked and consisted of loose material was bonded together by using a penetrating grout of epoxy resin; the ribs themselves were either rebuilt or secured in position by the use of long diagonal dowels of stainless steel. There were traces of mediaeval painting on the ceiling; these were restored and the bosses gilded at the expense of a private donor. It was the discovery of the potentially dangerous state of the ribs which underlined the necessity of the cleaning policy in the Minster.

In cleaning the Minster one could not help being struck by the contrast before and after. The internal appearance was changed substantially and the architectural form of the Minster became more apparent. The policy of painting the shadows in the bosses a heraldic red and gilding the highlights, which was initiated by Professor Sir Albert Richardson in the north and south transepts, was followed. Elsewhere it was intended that the pure form of the Minster should speak through the natural stone colour and the vaulting which was painted an off-white. This vaulting will inevitably darken a bit in time, but it has been insulated to prevent the pattern staining which has so disfigured other parts of the Minster. This insulation also conserves heat and saves fuel bills. After three bays at the east end had been cleaned, the trustees of the appeal agreed that the cleaning should continue down the whole length of the choir; because if the work was carried on in one operation, the cost of scaffolding would be greatly reduced. The Friends of the Minster kindly made themselves responsible for the gilding of the bosses, since the Dean and Chapter and the trustees did not feel they should divert money to purely decorative purposes.

CHAPTER SIX

CENTRAL TOWER FOUNDATIONS

RETURNING to the central tower foundations which constituted the major problem in the Minster, when the excavation was completed, a quarter of the new concrete foundation for each pier could be poured at a time. The first step was to pump out ground water and form a compression pad; then the Fressynet jacks were inserted, then the massive triangular concrete blocks which would form the new foundations were cast; and finally a collar round the base of the pier was cast. This process was repeated three times for each of the outside quarters. The inside quarter in the crossing area of the tower had a simple concrete retaining wall which would act as an anchorage for the tension bolts. Then the really challenging task of drilling began.

It took 9 months to drill some 50 holes in the north-west pier on the north-east south-west axis. Preliminary tests in sound Norman masonry had been encouraging, but it was found that the masonry under the pier was totally friable and in a semi-pulverised state. Diamond core drilling, which is slow and expensive, had to be used in order to secure a reasonably accurate alignment. Normally one can recover 90-95 per cent of a core, but in this instance the recovery was from 10-20 per cent. The water used to lubricate the drill had washed the other fragments away goodness knows where. But this confirmed our suspicions with regard to the inadequate nature of the existing foundations.

If a hole went off alignment it had to be filled in with grout and re-drilled. This could happen several times in one particular hole. Approximately 9,000 gallons of grout were pumped into that pier foundation over and above the preliminary grouting of the embedded Norman grillage. This grillage should be mentioned, as it was one of the early causes of concern for the stability of the central tower. Mr. Jesse Green, M.B.E. who served as clerk of works from 1930 to 1967 in a long and distinguished career, had discovered voids in the western crypt and had explored these some 90 feet to the west; thus it was known that these voids penetrated under the central tower piers. The consulting engineers and I were concerned about the possible collapse of the voids left by the grillage, so these were filled with gallons of grout. Grout for this purpose is a mixture of cement, fly ash and water inserted by hand pump with a pressure of up to 30 pounds per square foot generally. Higher pressures were allowed under the supervision of the resident engineer.

In the early exploration of the Minster the rotted remains of some of the large timbers were extracted wherever possible. I am glad to say that the voids had not collapsed, but the masonry had arched over successfully and left the shape of the original oak beams. These beams had rotted when the water table fell. The voids they had left were filled with concrete grout and this cause for concern was satisfactorily dealt with. However, not all fragments of the timber could be removed, and in certain instances embedded timber served to divert the drill from its proper course. Every type of drilling motion in the rotary and rotary percussive field was tried, and special bits were devised by Messrs. Holman, who helped greatly in this field, to meet the difficulty of drilling accurately in friable masonry horizontally. After nine months of perspiration and determination Messrs. Shepherd succeeded in completing one eighth of the total drilling task, and the reinforcing steel was placed and prestressed and grouted into position under the supervision of Norman Ross, the resident engineer, who wrote about the problems involved in drilling holes fifty feet long through the Norman foundations.

"The centres of the rods are 380 mm. (1 ft. 3 in.) apart horizontally and 450 mm. (1 ft. 6 in.) apart vertically in each direction. However, since one layer in each direction bisects the two layers in the orthogonal direction, the actual vertical distance between the layers is only 225 mm. (9 in.). From these figures it can be seen that the target after 12 to 15 m. (39 to 49 ft.) of drilling, allowing workable tolerances, is a rectangle only 300 x 225 mm. (1 ft. x 9 in.). Such accuracy has proved very difficult to achieve —perhaps not surprisingly.

The reason why drilling in the walls of the fabric was easier than in the foundations is not hard to find. Accurate drilling depends basically on two things:

1. The nature of the material being drilled.

2. The use of the correct equipment to suit the material.

The ideal material is a sound, homogeneous rock containing no fissures or voids. Mass concrete, of course, is equally acceptable. The degree by which a material departs from this standard is a measure of the difficulty one can expect in drilling through it. The Minster fabric, in the main, is well-bonded magnesian limestone masonry and, where rubble cores occur, they are well compacted and reasonably well mortared. On the other hand the Norman 'mortar raft' is far from ideal, for the following reasons:

a. It is non-homogeneous. The core has produced various limestones, red sandstone, millstone grits, a few igneous rocks, and even Roman tiles and bricks.

b. This miscellaneous rubble is held together by a matrix of lime/sand mortar, generally of a very low lime content. In parts the mortar is hard where presumably the proportions were better but usually it can be powdered between finger and thumb, presumably having undergone severe decomposition since it was first mixed in the 11th century. The soft mortar offers no resistance to the passage of the drill which can thus deflect easily when harder rocks are encountered. Also, since water is used to flush back the drilled material, small voids are often created when the soil mortar is also washed back. Prior to drilling, attempts were made at consolidating the 'mortar raft' by drilling holes for grout and pumping in a wet mix under pressure but, with few exceptions, only small 'takes' have been recorded. To improve the grout penetration *Pozament* is used at a water/cement ratio of about 0.6. *Pozament* is a proprietary cement consisting of roughly equal portions of pulverized fuel ash and ordinary Portland cement. The old mortar absorbs the water but not the solids. Experiments have also been made with epoxy resins as grout and excellent results have been achieved. There was excellent penetration of the mortar by the resin, producing a solid mass. Unfortunately the cost of using resins is prohibitive-blanket grouting of the existing foundations would cost approximately £500,000.

c. In the vicinity of each tower column the foundations have undergone differential settlements of up to 300 mm. (1 ft.). As a result they have fissured and deformed, producing shear planes which can deflect the drill from its correct alignment.

d. It was the practice of the Normans to reinforce their strip foundations with a continuous grillage of oak or elm baulks placed centrally. In the Minster the longitudinal members were 450 x 300 mm. (1 ft. 6 in. x 1 ft.) and the lateral 'distribution' members 300 x 300 mm. (1 ft. x 1 ft.). Much of the timber has rotted, leaving voids which have since been filled with sand/cement grout, but some has remained to provide yet another hindrance to easy drilling.

Compressed air drives most of the tools used on the Minster. Two Holman *Silver 3* percussive drills between them completed the work at high level on the towers. The bits used were 63 mm. (2.5 in.) diameter, with 'star' or 'cross' tungsten-carbide cutting heads. The drilling rods were hexagonal and hollow so that the flushing water could pass up through them to the cutting heads. The 32 mm. (1.3 in.) rods were standard and came in lengths of 1.2 m. (4 ft.). At regular intervals specially designed 63 mm. (2.5 in.) diameter couplers were used which fitted tightly to the hole yet allowed water and debris to pass through.

The same rigs were employed initially when the foundation drilling commenced. After a number of 'shots', most of which were badly off line, the situation was reviewed. The bits and drilling rods tended to feather which indicated that the rods were curving in profile. More powerful machines of the same type appeared to be the answer. The slightly larger *Silver 82* model and the *SL 16A* drifter were tested in turn. The drifter is a brute of a machine, very popular in mining engineering. At this stage also, experiments were carried out using other types of cutting heads namely 'button' bits and tri-cone or roller bits. In addition, all the conventional types and sizes of drilling rods and couplers were tested but without the success we were looking for. Even tube drilling was attempted on the percussive rig, using tubes for greater rigidity. The tubes we produced on the site failed miserably and even specially designed factory-made tubes could not withstand the stresses, especially fatigue, which this type of drilling sets up.

We now turned to diamond-core drilling which is both slow and expensive. The bits are hollow cylinders whose crowns consist of clusters of industrial diamonds set in a cobalt bed. Each bit costs about £70 and, on average, is good for only 61 m. (200 ft.) of drilling. The action is purely rotary as a percussive element would obviously smash the diamond crown. However it has proved to be at least one answer to the problem. It is accurate over long lengths through poor material because large diameter drilling tubes 75 mm. (3 in.) may be used. These are much less flexible than the 32 mm. (1.3 in.) diameter hexagonal rods used by the *Silver 3*. Even diamonds though, cannot drill through half-rotted timbers (the Norman reinforcement) and when these are encountered, fly-cutter bits or rag-bits have to be substituted for the diamond crown until the timber has been bored. Fly-cutters operate on the same principle as a carpenter's auger. On occasions a series of as many as five timbers has to be negotiated in this way in drilling just one hole.

The latest episode of the saga has been the successful introduction of the 'down-the-hole' vole hammer. This is a rotary-percussive tool which can be used on the same rig and with the same equipment as for the diamond coring. The percussive element is a hammer bit which has tungsten-carbide cutting edges. The vole hammer drills dry with compressed air passing up through the centre of the drilling tubes and forcing back the loosened material. The same air activates the percussive hammer.

This type of drilling has been accurate, quick and relatively inexpensive. Its secret lies in the stiffness of the drilling tubes and in the fact that the tubes are only required to transmit torque, all the percussion taking place at the cutting face.

While the work was in progress we were most concerned about the movement downward of the central tower. It was realised from the start that this was liable to happen and was in part due to the failure of the foundations and in part due to the urgent surgery which had to be carried out. An accurate record of the movements was kept and watched just as anxiously as the temperature of a feverish patient in hospital. It was noticeable that when the foundation had been contained by concrete the movements tended to slow down and when the stainless steel rods had been inserted movement was further reduced. The final operation to prevent any further movement was the inflation of the Fressynet jacks, of which more later.

The next pier to be drilled from the south-east to the north-west was the south-west pier. All the experience gained in the first operation was turned to good account in setting up this operation, and most of the work was carried out by a vole hammer on a rigid stem. This was both fast and accurate. In addition Ken Stephens, the contracts manager, arranged for more pre-grouting to be carried out. It is hard to know which factor affected the work most favourably, but the drilling was carried out in less than half the time it had taken to do the first pier.

In July 1970 the drills were set up to do the second set of reinforcement rods on the north-west pier working from the north-west to the south-east.

The difficulty of drilling had undoubtedly increased the cost of the restoration of the central tower foundations, as had also wage increases and the increases in the cost of raw materials, particularly stainless steel. Progress on the drilling was the key factor in completing the foundation work on the Minster, which it was hoped to achieve by April 1972. To ensure progress a night shift had been organised, and an electric compressor used so as to reduce noise and not to be a nuisance to the residents of Minster Yard. To stop all noise emanating from this compressor, it was enclosed with concrete blocks and a roof, and the result was satisfactory.

The foundation work of the central tower had always been the first priority; but other essential works were also carried out on it and one had the remarkable situation of simultaneous working on the roof and in the middle of the tower and in the foundations, and of letting the public have free access at main church floor level. This situation had to be watched carefully so that the safety of the public was ensured; but it was always regarded as an essential factor that the services in the Minster should not be interrupted. As Messrs. Shepherd's operatives trooped out at 3.55 p.m. the Choir assembled and Evensong started at 4.00 p.m. promptly. While Evensong was taking place, the workmen had their proper tea break; and provided that the psalms or Dr. Francis Jackson's anthem were not too long, they were back at work shortly after the statutory half hour pause. Work on the central tower superstructure was completed by the cleaning of the masonry and the reconstruction of the plaster ceiling with the restoration of the 15th century oak vaulting and bosses. Previously these bosses had been scarcely distinguishable or decipherable from the ground; but now having been gilded and painted at the expense of the Friends they were clearly visible when the scaffolding was struck. The original bosses which had survived the fires of 1829 and 1840 were found to be of a powerful simplified design. Whether this was a conscious revival of Norman style, or whether it was the artists' simplification so as to read from a great height it is difficult to decide; but the fact remains that the bosses are most effective sculptures. The most striking is the central boss of St. Peter and St. Paul, the former with his crossed keys holding the Church which is being defended by the latter with a drawn sword. The bosses, representing the four Evangelists' symbols, can be seen at the main junctions of the vault at midspan; the remainder probably represent four bishops and the twelve apostles, one of whom is upside down and two-headed—could this possibly be Judas?

At the west end an exploratory dig was made; and this confirmed our suspicion that the problems of foundations would be similar to those of the central tower. Based on two years' knowledge and study of the peculiar conditions of the Minster, Messrs. Arup recommended that our original ideas should be somewhat expanded and that the foundations which had been proposed for the freestanding piers should also include the external walls and buttresses in order to include the whole of each tower in one foundation system. Mr. Potter concurred in this, I as surveyor agreed, and the trustees approved the proposal. Preliminary excavation was started in April 1970 in order to give the archaeologists more time for their studies. Almost immediately they discovered western towers dating from the 12th century and other unusual features of the Norman Minster. This work was assisted by the installation of mechanical elevators. There was also a large and welcome increase in the volunteer archaeological force.

The north-west tower had already been strengthened by the insertion of girdles at three levels and had been thoroughly consolidated with the insertion of 3,500 gallons of grout. The stone was then restored by the Minster masons and all masonry pointing carefully attended to. The stonework was also washed. Then the south-west tower was scaffolded in order that the stainless steel girdles could be inserted to secure this structure against the major cracks which had weakened each tower.

CHAPTER SEVEN

PROGRAMMING AND MANAGEMENT

FROM 1970 onwards, when the problems of drilling had been overcome, it became possible to institute sophisticated programming. Initially I had estimated that some 80 men would be required to work on the Minster and I had produced a bar chart to show priorities and targets. This chart was rather optimistic and had to be revised. But who in the building industry is not an optimist when making target programmes? However, with the complex problems ahead of us, it would have been irresponsible not to try and programme them properly. This was not a normal job and often the programmer had difficulty in understanding the full engineering significance of the proposed sequence of operations. Ove Arup and Partners had to review the draft programme in order to amend this aspect of the work.

Network planning was introduced, as an effective way of expressing the method and sequence of the various activities showing their interrelation with one another in both particular and parallel phases of the work. Through this network one could assess the critical path of the work and it was clear that drilling would determine the completion date. Accordingly, the drilling programme was studied separately and a graph set up in the contractor's site hut which showed progress with the number of holes completed plotted against time elapsed. At first progress was not too good; but when the noisy diesel compressor (called the 'red devil') was superseded by an electric compressor which could be run at night without disturbing every one in the vicinity, it became possible to institute a night shift. Additional drilling plant was authorised to enable more men to work at one time and by the combination of working on a wider front for longer hours, the drilling programme was brought back by July 1970 within the overall target programme. I promised Ken Stephens a bottle of high proof malt whisky when the rate of drilling exceeded the target. Unfortunately progress hovered just below the line for a rather long time and I drank the special whisky myself; but shortly before Christmas 1970 drilling crossed the line and Ken received his well deserved bottle, having acquired rather a thirst by that time.

Now, with the right equipment and powerful drills it was possible for one team to drill a hole through 50 feet of masonry and concrete in two hours. That would be a "good" hole but a bad hole might take eight hours. But in order to obtain the requisite accuracy a hole might have to be drilled two or three times or even up to eight times. Nevertheless, with a combination of "down-the-hole" vole percussive drills, diamond corers, wood augers and a wide range of bits the drilling teams, who had by now acquired the special know-how of the job that makes all the difference, were able to keep up and exceed our programme. The last hole in the central tower was drilled on December 17th 1971 and the Dean and Chapter wrote a letter congratulating Messrs. Shepherd on this event.

Network planning with a critical path provides a detailed effective control for all levels of management engaged on building work. The network is presented in the form of an arrowed diagram supported by computer data which enables the progress of the work to be monitored and also expresses the duration and timing of each and every operation, high lighting those activities which are critical. The method gives a comprehensive evaluation of the whole project; and when materials have been quantified, it enables the requirements of labour and other resources to be estimated. In its application it constitutes a record of performance and gives a complete forecast of future events. In setting up computerised programming we might also have included computerised costing of the work, for after all the computer was dealing with labour materials and time; and these could also have been costed to give forecasts of the total cost of the work. However, unfortunately, this opportunity was not anticipated but I am mentioning it in case another similar project occurs.

The chart is a diary of past events and a forecast for future work. Most important of all it gives the implications of deviations from the programme, which is valuable in building contracts suffering as they do from unforeseen events besides rain and the weather and the possibility of the shortage of materials.

On York Minster, we were protected from the rain internally and took very adequate precautions to protect the external works; but we had another hazard which occurred rather unexpectedly to upset the programming of the works. This was the hazard of archaeological finds. Time and time again the surveyor had to evaluate the claims of archaeology and study the programme to see how a delay here might be overcome by working in a different place. Ken Stephens was always understanding and helpful, although some of the concessions he agreed to must have cost him dear.

After much consultation an improved programme was devised for the central tower section and rather more time was allowed for the interrelated operations. In the overall programme, plant is a major limiting factor and additional drilling plant and other specialised equipment had to be purchased. But the use and movement of scaffolding was particularly complex. Some 30,000 feet of scaffolding had been bought so as to avoid hire charges which would have been considerable over a period of seven years. In fact this scaffolding was used eight times over. It is certain that the hire charges would have been much greater than the purchase cost; and in the event the resale of the surplus scaffolding at the end of this work was a useful bonus to offset some unexpected extra costs. Poul Beckmann and I supported the contractor's efforts to programme the work properly and Ken Stephens was assisted by Brian Pearson as programming clerk.

At this stage the organisation of the contractor was reviewed by Poul Beckmann and myself; and we felt that perhaps there was some difficulty in conveying the subtle engineering aspects of the job to the contractor. This is no criticism of anyone. The simplest solution would have been to ask Messrs. Shepherd to appoint a contract engineer. However, this would have upset the balance of the team and it was decided that we must ask Norman Ross, the resident engineer, to take on some extra responsibilities which normally would have fallen on the contractor's shoulders. He undertook to do a good deal more setting out, which could be taken in with his own routine survey checks. Part of the flexibility of the work arose from having a first rate resident engineer who was able to make quick and responsible decisions and could communicate in a friendly way with the contractor.

Frequently Norman Ross had to do a considerable amount of redesign of reinforcement so that archaeological finds could be retained in position. He and I watched the chart of the downward movements of the piers very carefully each week and these were reported at regular quarterly intervals to the trustees. It was a difficult business standing by and knowing that the central tower was going down at an unexpectedly high rate. Yet, as reported initially, the question was whether the fabric was strong enough to stand this surgery. We knew we had adopted the kindest and most conservative type of repair possible. Once a pier had been cased in concrete the imponderable danger of damage by bursting sideways had been removed; then the problem was one simply of settlement. Settlement in itself could not damage the central tower so much but would have a bad effect on the adjacent parts of the Minster. Therefore, Norman Ross and myself watched these areas very carefully.

When it became apparent that the settlement was continuing, it was decided to erect fan boards in order to protect the public against the possibility of stone falling. A small amount of stone did fall; and the triforium arches in the north and south transepts also suffered a certain amount of distress. Early in 1971 I made a complete check of the areas adjacent to the central tower and was gratified to find that the damage was confined to the reopening of old cracks and did not appear to be nearly as bad as might have been expected. However, the daily supervision of the resident engineer was a vital element in the whole organisation of the repair works.

In the winter of 1970 and 1971 when it was possible to extend operations down the choir working from the east end, the foundations of each pier were exposed and if necessary improved. Exposure involved archaeological excavations. In several cases enlargement of the mediaeval foundations was found to be necessary and this was done by bonding the new concrete to the old masonry with dowels. For these piers it was not considered necessary to introduce the more complicated concept of compression pad. When opening up the columns in the eastern crypt where recent downward movement had been noticed I was very surprised to find one of the 14th century columns resting on only half a foundation. This prompted my comment at a press conference that this foundation work was a piece of mediaeval "jerry-building". Unfortunately, the comment was misinterpreted by the national newspapers as being applied to York Minster as a whole, and the *Daily Sketch* gave me the honourable award for the stupidest saying of the week.

In 1970 all those connected with the Minster and the appeal suffered a great loss in the death of Lord Scarbrough. Lord Scarbrough was one of the greatest men of his age. He could command the loyalties of every type of man and had caused miners, farmers, citizens of all type and class to come to the support of the Minster. He was respected and influential in every circle and to his talents must go a large share of the credit for raising the £2 million required.

We all gathered in the nave for his memorial service, at which both the Queen and Queen Mother were represented as well as 26 local authorities. By his explicit instructions there was to be no address and his name was only mentioned once. Those of us who loved and respected him were sad that no verbal tribute could be given. But as the twelfth Earl said, his father had sat though so many bad addresses that he was determined that none should be given for him. The Dean and Chapter thought of a suitable memorial to the great service that Lord Scarbrough had given to the Minster and instructed me to design a memorial slab to go under the central tower with the wording 'In Memory of Roger Lawrence Lumley 11th Earl of Scarbrough KG together with those whose efforts have saved this central tower'.[1]

Lord Scarbrough had been Grand Master of the Freemasons of England for many years and had only recently handed over that office to his Royal Highness the Duke of Kent, becoming himself ProGrand Master. It was therefore not surprising that the Grand Lodge of England should also wish to commemorate Lord Scarbrough in some way in the Minster. This was done in July 1971 when the Rose Window in the south transept, which had been restored with some special features, was rededicated in his memory.

1. The stone was carved by York Minster stonemasons and laid on St. Peter's Day, June 29th, 1972 on the second anniversary of his death. It was dedicated by the Archbishop of York at a great Service of Thanksgiving.

CHAPTER EIGHT

THE STAINED GLASS AND WESTERN TOWERS

NOW it is expedient to discuss the restoration of stained glass which was carried out concurrently with the main work. In 1969 the Pilgrim Trust through Lord Kilmain as secretary had agreed with the Dean and Chapter to establish the York Glaziers Trust. A grant of nearly £6,000 was given towards the conversion of the upper floor of the north wing of the Stoneyard quarters for glaziers; and additional working capital was made available. Special benches were provided with perspex tops and light underneath so that the glaziers could see their work as they did it. The perspex itself was perforated by a grid of small holes at close centres like an accoustic tile so that the glaziers could stick their nails in to hold glass in position. Special racks to store glass and dipping tanks to wash glass were made, and with the guidance of Mr. Denis King of Norwich, an ultrasonic cleaning tank was purchased and glass polishing equipment was installed. The glaziers were led at first by Bob Lazenby. On his retirement in 1970 he was succeeded as superintendent by Peter Gibson. Having been provided with a good workshop the Glaziers Trust was in a position to expand its activities, the basic strategy of which was to use the work on York Minster as a "fly-wheel" but to take in as much external work as possible with the backing of the Council for the Care of Churches and the Pilgrim Trust. Grants were obtainable for the restoration of historic glass in the possession of parishes for work to be carried out by the Trust.

For a part of 1971 and the whole of 1972 the resources of the Trust were devoted entirely to work on the Minster, due to the exigencies of the restoration programme which was scheduled to follow the cleaning work from the east end to the west end. It was decided to wash and overhaul all the glass as and when possible from the scaffolding. Defective glass in the tracery lights of windows in the choir aisles was replaced and the opportunity taken to improve the design and incorporate the coats of arms of the trustees of the York Minster fund and some of armigerii members of the High Steward's committee. This followed a mediaeval precedent of saying 'Thank you' to benefactors by displaying their arms; and it is to be hoped that this precedent will continue. The arms of the Deanery and the See have been included together with those of Lord Scarbrough, Lord Normanby, Brigadier Hargreaves, Mr. Marcus Worsley, Mr. Gibbs, Mr. Cobb, Colonel Upton, Mr. Crosse, and Mr. Roscoe. All these shields were prepared from known coats of arms by Dr. Eric Gee and executed by Mr. Denis King's workshop in Norwich. Mr. King also kindly gave the glass in the easternmost window of the north choir aisle which matches and completes the scheme devised by Dean Milner White for this window. There was, however, no time to reglaze the windows in the clerestory close to the east end; so these had to be left and were merely stippled over with paint to adjust the level of luminosity to the correct degree.

At that time besides the contractors, painters and decorators who were scrubbing the stone, painting the ceiling, and gilding the bosses, we had masons carrying out necessary repairs, plasterers repairing the plaster, and glaziers all working on the complicated co-ordinated programme to complete the overhaul of the internal surfaces of the Minster.

Now to return to the structural works. In April 1970 it was decided that the western towers should be started in good time so as to give the archaeologists an opportunity to do their work properly The digging by the archaeologists was to be mechanised by the introduction of conveyor belts and was costed against target. The greatest care was taken to plan this work so as to avoid the difficulties which had caused frustration previously. Work was to start on the south-west tower and go round to the north-west. This involved reducing the width of Deangate; and Ken Stephens organised a fantastic weekend operation, by which half Deangate was dug up, planked over with heavy precast concrete beams and then resurfaced to provide the working space necessary for digging and drilling the foundations without totally closing the road. It was found necessary to divert quite large rainwater conduits as well. Despite heavy rain over the weekend the operation was efficiently carried out.

Very complex archaeological problems were uncovered in this area which had belonged to the first cohort of the sixth "Varia Victrix" legion. Several levels of Roman occupation posed complicated archaeological problems and in addition the continuous use of these buildings by the Saxons added to the complications.

A great deal of the digging was carried out below the cost target; but in some areas the cost was nearly three times the average. This would occur where a small amount had to be removed under difficult conditions: but the overall cost of the excavation was only slightly above the target of £5 per cubic yard, which is not excessive for work under difficult conditions.

The first structural difficulty was met when a quite severe crack was found in the north-east column of the south-west tower. For safety this had to be collared with reinforced concrete immediately. Work proceeded to a pre-arranged plan; but Arup found it necessary to enlarge the size of the foundations which were designed to spread the loads of the two western towers adequately.

Work in one vital area was delayed two months because the archaeologist digging it was ill—an awkward situation for Derek Phillips who did not wish to transfer the work to another person and so lose continuity. By July 1970, with archaeological funds running low, a difficult decision had to be made; and the archaeologists were warned that no further delay could be permitted, particularly as the contractors wished to speed up their programme.

However, the Minster herself refused to allow the speedier programme to be put into effect, as the record of measurements showed an unexpected outward movement of both western towers. It was necessary to take the precaution of putting up shores—the same shores which had been taken from the east-end and laid near the west-end in readiness for such a possible emergency. These were brought into action immediately; and within a month the rather ominous movements had been arrested and work could proceed again. This diversion gave valuable time to the archaeologists, who by then had also received a further grant enabling them to continue. Since it was clear that the condition of the Minster would not permit work to proceed on the proposed fast programme, the archaeologists continued to finish their work in this area, finally working round the clock and stopping on Wednesday January 19th 1972 at 7.15 a.m. The contractors moved into the area exactly fifteen minutes later.

The design for foundations of the western towers was similar to that used for the central tower but rather simpler; only one layer of rods was necessary and no diagonal drilling was required. Details of reinforcement were devised so as to minimise the amount of drilling through concrete; and after the stainless steel rods had been inserted and tensioned, large amounts of concrete were cast in the open castellations left for this purpose. The final result was a unified foundation for the external walls of each tower and the related nave pier, this pier being one of the heaviest loaded members in the whole Minster. Early in the restoration the upper part of the north-west tower had been strengthened by the insertion of three girdles of stainless steel ties. The same procedure was now adopted for the south-west tower. This meant putting up scaffolding to the top of the tower, so the opportunity was taken to wash the tower overall followed by repointing the masonry with particular care. The scaffolding on this tower however was urgently needed at the end of October for the cleaning of the nave; and as the maintenance work proceeded the scaffolding was taken down and moved into the nave and re-erected. The final section of scaffolding was removed from the nave in March 1972.

CHAPTER NINE

COMPLETION

ON the central tower, after the crisis of drilling had been solved, the main problem was simply to get through the large amount of work involved. The procedure of excavation, strutting, sandbagging, setting up reinforcement, shuttering, casting concrete with tubes in for the future holes, and drilling followed a well-defined routine until we came to the south-east pier, where the design had to be modified fundamentally because a large mass of Norman masonry was encountered. As we could incorporate this masonry into our new design, there seemed no point in taking the risk of removing it in order to replace it with concrete; so a low level tunnel, twelve feet below floor level, was driven in a north-easterly direction from the south transept through into the south choir aisle. Then the concrete anchorages were cast and the holes drilled from a north westerly direction. This large mass of Roger's church can be seen by serious students of architectural history or archaeology. Certain parts of Thomas' church were also exposed; and access can be gained to view this from a manhole cover left in the floor of the store in the angle between the choir and south transept. There are in addition two areas of rather interesting Norman masonry which can be reached by lifting a loose slab of stone set in the floor of the south choir aisle.

In fact the movements on the south-east pier were some of the worst we had experienced: and my original forecast that this would be the most difficult pier to reconstitute was realised—somewhat to the surprise of the resident engineer, who asked me how I had come to that conclusion three years earlier. I answered that it was by looking at it.

Having succeeded with the drilling of the north-west pier the reinforcing rods were threaded through, anchored and tightened up with hydraulic jacks to a load of 33 pounds per square inch. After they had been under this tension for two months their stressing was rechecked, and if necessary they were tightened further. When we had stabilised the tension in the rods, they were then grouted; and one could say with confidence that new work was securely bonded to the old. Having achieved this state, the last phase of the foundation work could be put into effect. The hydraulic cells were connected up to a hand pump filled with fluid and the slow process of raising the pressure of the Fressynet jack under both north-west and south-west piers was started. First pressure was taken up to 500 pounds per square inch and no movement was recorded; at 1,000 pounds per square inch a small amount of movement was recorded; at 1,500 pounds per square inch movements ranging from $\frac{1}{2}$ inch to $1\frac{1}{2}$ inches were recorded and about 7 out of the 100 hydraulic cells failed. This was unfortunate but not of vital significance, as some could be replaced. Then when movements had ceased, the space created by expanding the hydraulic cells was filled with grout so that the piers rested on solid foundations, grout replacing the jacks as load carrying members. In doing this we found we had overlooked one simple practical point—that it would have been much easier to fill this void if it had been six inches above floor level rather than two inches below. The consulting engineer's idea of inflating the hydraulic cells in order to share the load between the new and the old foundations and to remove all traces of eccentricity in the foundations had been a triumphant success; and the central tower had even moved upwards a fraction of an inch.

By studying the relative movements, it was decided that it was possible to start reinstating the floor of the Minster without risk of cracking the new structure. This was done by casting the coffer slabs which now form the ceiling of the undercroft and then laying the stone paving, restoring the pattern designed by Lord Burlington and William Kent. I had asked Messrs. Arup if they could design a floor slab without intermediate columns. The coffer construction was the ideal answer, as it had an attractive undersurface and could span large distances, i.e., 45 feet without more support than provided at the edges.

The slabs present an attractive pattern when seen from below and reflect light in a variety of ways; and the detailing was designed to give the effect of a floating ceiling by forming a deep groove round the perimeter. However, visitors to the Minster were vastly puzzled by the white bath tubs which appeared on top of the shuttering of the ceiling, these bath tubs being the reverse form of the coffers.

The floor was cast working from the nave round through the K.O.Y.L.I. chapel, north transept, central crossing and finally the south transept. Plain concrete slabs were used in the north and south nave aisles and under the choir steps.

The execution of the work under the choir had been particularly difficult, as this involved underpinning the choir screen with additionally a diagonal cut in and under the Norman retaining walls to secure anchorages for the reinforcement. When this work had been done it was possible to reinstate the nineteenth century arches and begin the formation of the proposed treasury. A void was left in the treasury floor so that visitors could look down at the remains of the Roman legionary commandant's house. This void created a difficulty as there was one arch resting upon a column which would have had to run down and rest on the floor of the lower chamber. This seemed a clumsy arrangement; but it was desirable to maintain the rhythm of the arches, so this arch was hung from a concealed steel beam set in the masonry above. This was an architectural joke; but Ken Stephens told some serious minded engineering students, "Although it is not in the text books if you build an arch properly you could do that which, as it appears, defies the laws of gravity". This statement caused some puzzlement but none of them thought of looking underneath the arch to see the steel plate that held the stone in position.

Having reinstated the structural floor, it was then possible to install the new mechanical and electrical services which are so necessary for a cathedral in the twentieth century—for it can be said that an historic building is only as old as its mechanical and electrical services. We had already installed modern boilers; but these had never been worked to capacity because they could not develop their full pressure until all the building work was completed. Heating mains had to be run round the Minster and up into the triforium; air conditioning trunking had to be run across the floor of the treasury and up into the voids beneath the seats of the choir; compressed air supplies for the engineering works and for future repairs had to be run round the Minster; and the whole electrical installation had to be revised. The electrical consultants, in particular Charles Eaves, and the heating consultants, Mr. Jennings and

Ray Turner, have my sympathy for their patience; simply because it was impossible to brief them at an early date about all the problems of the job, because we could have no accurate drawings until the work was done. However, by close co-operation they have achieved a neat job; and the heating in the Minster has been improved by low-level convectors in the nave and a blanket of warm air at high-level and the supply of humidified air to the choir where it is hoped to build up a small positive air pressure in order to reduce the amount of draughts. At the same time the Zouche Chapel and the Chapter House were brought into the scheme of things.

The electric installation involved a new 300 kw transformer and new main and sub-distribution boards; but it has not been possible to complete the lighting scheme because it was decided to wait until the effect of the "Son et Lumière" lighting had been studied. However, additional light was provided in the area of the high altar, and certain experiments were made to find fittings that were powerful enough to give the requisite amount of light in the Minster. Provision for the "Son et Lumière" installation came under Charles Eaves, and a very sophisticated electronic control centre has been established under the north choir aisle. The Standard Telephone Company have advised on the improvement of the sound reinforcement scheme; and a new console has been tucked in under the organ by the entrance to the choir, while new speakers have been installed in the choir. These are designed to be good for voice reinforcement; but additional equipment is required for music, as in "Son et Lumière". All these complicated services required an immense amount of care to install so that they were almost invisible; and this was the detailed responsibility of Norman Lister and Neil Birdsall of my office.

After the electrical and mechanical services had been installed it was possible to start the reinstatement of the paving in the Minster. For some time Bill Holland, the mason foreman, had foreseen this problem and had been sawing up slabs in the stoneyard and setting them aside in readiness. He had already obtained a second-hand planing machine with the express object of resurfacing the stones which we had taken out initially, and this proved to be invaluable.

The paviors had earlier reinstated the area of the central crossing. This may sound a simple job; but the pattern laid down in the eighteenth century had to be followed meticulously with one exception—the insertion of a new memorial stone for Lord Scarbrough in the centre under the central tower. Then there were difficulties in getting enough large blocks of stone from the quarry to make paving. An agreement had been made with Messrs. Tilcon in 1969 to extract 10,000 cubic feet of stone from the original Huddestone stone quarry which had supplied the original stone for the Minster. This had been reopened by kind permission of Mr. Hawking, but not without difficulty, because over-burden had to be removed and an access road formed. The good stone beds were located, but there were great difficulties in extracting the stone; and Messrs. Tilcons' patience and business integrity in honouring a difficult contract was much to be admired. One of the difficulties was that the large blocks tended to come out wedge shaped and were therefore not so good for use as paving as might have been hoped, although they would be perfectly adequate for producing small ashlar stones. However, in my opinion it is absolutely essential to get the right stone to preserve the harmony of the building as a whole; and although there may have been difficulties in opening the quarry and getting the stone out, it was well worthwhile. But the problem was a nice one—how long could we manage to keep up with the programme of works with this difficult supply situation? It is for this reason that the reinstatement of the stone paving at the west end was delayed somewhat and concrete slabs used as a temporary measure.

In the autumn of 1971 we were ready for the last phase of the internal work: the cleaning of the nave. It had been hoped to start this in September, but the starting date was postponed until October 27th so as to allow the schoolchildren of York to take part in a magnificent spectacle called "The Worldmakers". Shortly afterwards we learned that the Queen might be visiting York Minster for the Royal Maundy; and although this was not official we realised that our plans might have to be accelerated. Ken Stephens worked out his plans for moving the scaffolding from east to west.

At first he wanted to hire scaffolding in order to get an earlier start, but I said this could not be afforded; so we had to collect scaffolding from all corners of the job and get as much as possible from the southwest tower. As the scaffolding came down from the tower, it went up in the nave. Three great piers of scaffolding were erected and these were braced diagonally and met at the apex of the roof to form a working platform for the painters and decorators who dusted, scrubbed and cleaned the stone, returning it to its original colour and texture. The workmen looked like pygmies in this vast jungle of scaffolding. As before, the vaulting was painted "off white" and the bosses painted and gilded on a heraldic red ground. However, an exception was made for the eight central bosses. These are in fact mid-nineteenth century copies of the earlier Gothic bosses which had been recorded by John Browne. Here, on the advice of Lord Clark, we decided to paint the ground of the boss in a light blue colour and I think this appropriately emphasises and links the sequence of magnificent bosses which are in the honour of the Virgin Mary. With the contractor's programme setting the pace, it was necessary to get both glaziers and masons to keep in step. For the masons this was difficult at first, as there were several problems to be sorted out, particularly on the north-west side of the northwest central pier, where an arch and part of a vault had to be rebuilt and several ribs reinstated. One of these ribs was so precarious that when I touched the arch vousoir[1] it moved but it was caught in time and did not fall. In re-forming the vaulting, an earlier area of Norman wall was discovered, and this had a small blind window which was embedded in the nave arcade.

On the south side there was less work to do; but in the third bay we found that part of one of the main choir arcade arches had slipped. This was lifted back into position using hydraulic props and then the arch was bodily refixed by the masons. One missing boss on the north side was recreated in fibreglass and painted and gilded so that it was indistinguishable from the remainder. This technique saved a delay of at least a fortnight which we could not have afforded.

During the preliminary planning of the nave cleaning I had frankly not believed that the glaziers could keep up with the programme. However, I discussed it with Peter Gibson, the superintendent, and Denis King as consultant. The task was to restore fully the two windows adjacent to the central

1. Vousoir is one of the curved stones forming an arch.

tower which also involved masonry work, to reglaze all the tracery lights down each side of the nave, and to restore one of the major windows at the west end. In addition, one of the choir windows immediately above the Dean's stall had to be refixed. Never before had the glaziers been asked to tackle such a task, nor co-ordinate their work so closely with that of an outside contractor. However, Peter Gibson was game.

We first had to decide on the aesthetic and technical solutions of the glazing to the clerestory. Here we had three or four conferences under the chairmanship of Canon Burbridge and obtained the advice of Dr. Newton and Mr. Denis King. Examples were offered and adjusted and finally the tracery was reglazed; but we were not entirely satisfied. Then Dr. Newton suggested more colour in the centre of the larger panels and this suggestion was adopted.

The object of this glazing programme was threefold: first, to use the scaffolding provided by the contractor and to save further scaffolding costs; secondly, to extract all the fragments of beautiful twelfth century glass which had been inserted at random and which might contain the elements of window panels which Dr. Newton might be able to reassemble; thirdly, an important aesthetic objective, to provide more light through the tracery glass of the nave in order to "lift" the vault. We also wanted a consistent treatment and to get rid of the temporary black panels which had been in these windows for the last twenty-five years. These had disfigured the Minster and prevented people from appreciating the light and beauty of the nave. In the future, when we have to take out glass, we propose to insert appropriate temporary glazing and not leave black panels.

There are nine different sorts of design of grissaile glass in these clerestory windows, and samples of these were worked out by Peter Gibson. Having established design and standards, we felt able to call in the help of the M.A.G. Glazing Company to take some of the burden of this pressing programme off the shoulders of the York Glaziers Trust. In this way, despite a somewhat delayed start, the programme was achieved by an earlier finishing date than had been anticipated. With the magnificent co-operation of the contractors, the Queen's Royal Maundy visit was made possible; only a small amount of scaffolding in the last bay of the nave and the last two bays of the aisles at the west end was left on March 28th, 1972.

As the scaffolding approached the west end, we met a problem we had not anticipated. The old seventeenth century "fleet"[1] had become surrounded by scaffolding—there was no way of getting it out nor was there any safe way of incorporating it into the scaffolding. This was reported to the Dean and Chapter, who reluctantly agreed that it should be dismantled and stored in the space formed in between the foundations at the west end. This space is envisaged as a chair store as well as a store for the platforms on which visiting orchestras and choirs have to be seated. It must be appreciated that York Minster with seating for 2,500 people, is the best concert hall that York is likely to have in the foreseeable future.

The undercroft under the central tower had evolved into a scheme for telling the story of York Minster in relation to York, England and Europe. As a result of the archaeological excavations, upstanding Roman walls had

1. The fleet is a ladder plus working stage on a set of four wheels. In effect rather like a mediaeval siege tower.

been left in position so that their meaning and significance could be explained. There was also remains of the 1st Cohort barracks at the west end. Plaster which had fallen from one of these walls had been delicately and patiently pieced together by Mr. Norman Davey who is a genius at this sort of work.

He had spent over three years on this labour of love and the plaster was finally re-erected in the undercroft in March 1972 within a few feet of its original situation in the 3rd century A.D. This plaster shows a Pompeian type wall painting with a column set upon a plinth and a frieze having dramatic masques and a bird flying through the sky between the columns; it measures about 18 feet by 10 feet. In spite of large gaps, it gives a remarkable insight into the standard of the furnishing of the legionary fortress.

Thinking in terms of an almost continuous snake of people moving at an average speed of about half a mile an hour, it is hoped to give visitors a kinetic display using projection and sound effects to tell part of the story. In the meantime use was made of the means ready at hand to provide an interesting script and explain the significance of the exhibits. This enterprise is very necessary in order to help raise funds for the maintenance of the Minster. It was made possible by a generous gift from the Wolfson Foundation and from the Esmee Fairbairn Trust; and it is linked to the Treasury, which was also made possible by an equally generous grant from the Worshipful Company of Goldsmiths. Ideally one should have been given £20,000 for display and two years for preparation. In fact, I had just about £2,000 and two months with the help of my staff to get this ready.

The fascination of the display is that you are dealing with living history and that you have the contrasts of the first century with the twentieth. You walk where the Emperors Hadrian, Septimus Severus, Constantius Chlorus and Constantine the Great walked. You are on the site where Constantine was proclaimed Emperor and set out to establish his claim by force of arms. You are near where King Arthur, if he existed, celebrated the first Christmas in England. And you have the contrast of the four great piers each carrying 4,000 tons coming down through the ceiling and resting on the new foundations which have been pressed into the earth by hydraulic cells. All this has to be made intelligible and explained to the man in the street, whose contributions will help preserve the Minster for the future.

The last but not the least item which had to be considered in order to restore the Minster to normal was the great organ. This is one of the largest organs in Britain and has magnificent pipes, the largest of which are 32 feet in length, made of cast lead and weighing 1½ tons. Being of lead they have to be carried extremely carefully in case they collapse under their own weight. Messrs. J. W. Walker & Sons are the organ builders responsible and they have co-operated valiantly and patiently with various stages of reinstatement. A cathedral organ costs tens of thousands of pounds and has to be treated with extreme care where dust and humidity are concerned. New organ blowers were necessary and it was expedient to re-arrange some of the ranks of pipes in order to improve their sound output; but cost considerations prevented any improvements which it might have been tempting to suggest.

Particularly in restoration works, cost budgeting always has to be strictly observed. However, the re-arrangement of pipes gave space for an improved staircase to be created and a new music store was built for the cathedral music with over 300 feet run of shelving in a place readily accessible to the choir.

CHAPTER TEN

COST CONTROL

THE Dean and Chapter, who are responsible for York Minster, delegated financial control of the appeal work to the trustees of the York Minster Fund. Although the Dean sat upon the body as a trustee, any proposed work had to have the approval of both bodies. When an item of work was proposed a budget price was set on it and approved. Costs were allocated monthly by Frank Hall, the quantity surveyor, according to work done under each heading and the balance of the budget reported. These were then reported quarterly when the surveyor to the fabric and quantity surveyor to the appeal reported to the trustees. Due to the inherent difficulties of the work and its unique nature, the making of estimates was extraordinarily difficult. Costs and trends had to be studied in detail and kept constantly under review in order to ensure that all first priority work was carried out.

The fund raising costs of the appeal were kept remarkably low, as were the administrative costs and professional fees. All the professional consultants were retained on a time basis, and in this way they made a contribution to the York Minster appeal.

The over-riding consideration in the organisation of work was of course to get value for money. This was obtained, first by organising the work efficiently; secondly using as much plant as possible to save labour; thirdly ensuring the steady flow of materials; and lastly ensuring good communications, so that decisions were always made sufficiently in advance of the event. To study the efficiency of the operation comparative graphs were kept of the cost of labour, the cost of materials, the cost of plant, the work sub-contracted and builder's fees. It is a remarkable fact that for the duration of the major part of the contract labour costs were less than that of materials. Normally on restoration work one expects the opposite.

My initial estimates for the cost of the work were £1.67 million to £2.5 million; and it was Lord Scarbrough who decided the appeal should be for £2 million. The actual cost for the work which I budgeted for in the appeal was about £2.25 million; but by postponing the less urgent but necessary roof works we were able to bring the total appeal work within the £2 million target. When making my estimates I took no account of inflation, and on average this raised the cost of the appeal work by 10% each year. It is also an interesting fact that the cost of restoration work normally tends to go up more quickly than average building costs simply because the labour content is very high. Here is a summary of estimates and final costs.

A simplified comparison of Gross Costs as at 1st January 1974 with Estimated Costs given in January 1967:—

	Gross estimated as at January 1967	Actual as at 1st January 74
Central Tower	450,000-930,000	713,000
East End & Choir Piers	120,000-140,000	103,000
North West Tower including shores	300,000-430,000	237,000
South West Tower including shores	300,000-430,000	237,000
Roof Repairs & Insulation	138,000-155,000 (Works not completed)	79,000

	Gross estimated as at January 1967	Actual as at 1st January 74
Engineering Services	50,000-59,000	102,000
Organ Reinstatement	10,500-13,000	24,000
Miscellaneous Building Work	69,000-77,000	83,000
Cleaning & Scaffolding	69,000-80,000	89,000
Undercroft & Treasury	(not included)	24,000
Stoneyard & Glaziers	210,000-245,000	366,000
Archaeology	15,000-18,000	7,500

*A further sum of £47,809 was provided by grants from the Dept. of the Environment, the British Academy, the Pilgrim Trust, the Russell Trust and the Leverhulme Trust. The cost of writing up is estimated to be over £40,000, and will take up at least five years.

To arrive at Gross Costs, Administrative Costs of £62,000 approx., Professional Fees at £189,000 approx. and Direct Costs of £36,000 have been allocated on a percentage basis of 11.6% to the Actual Costs as at December 1973.

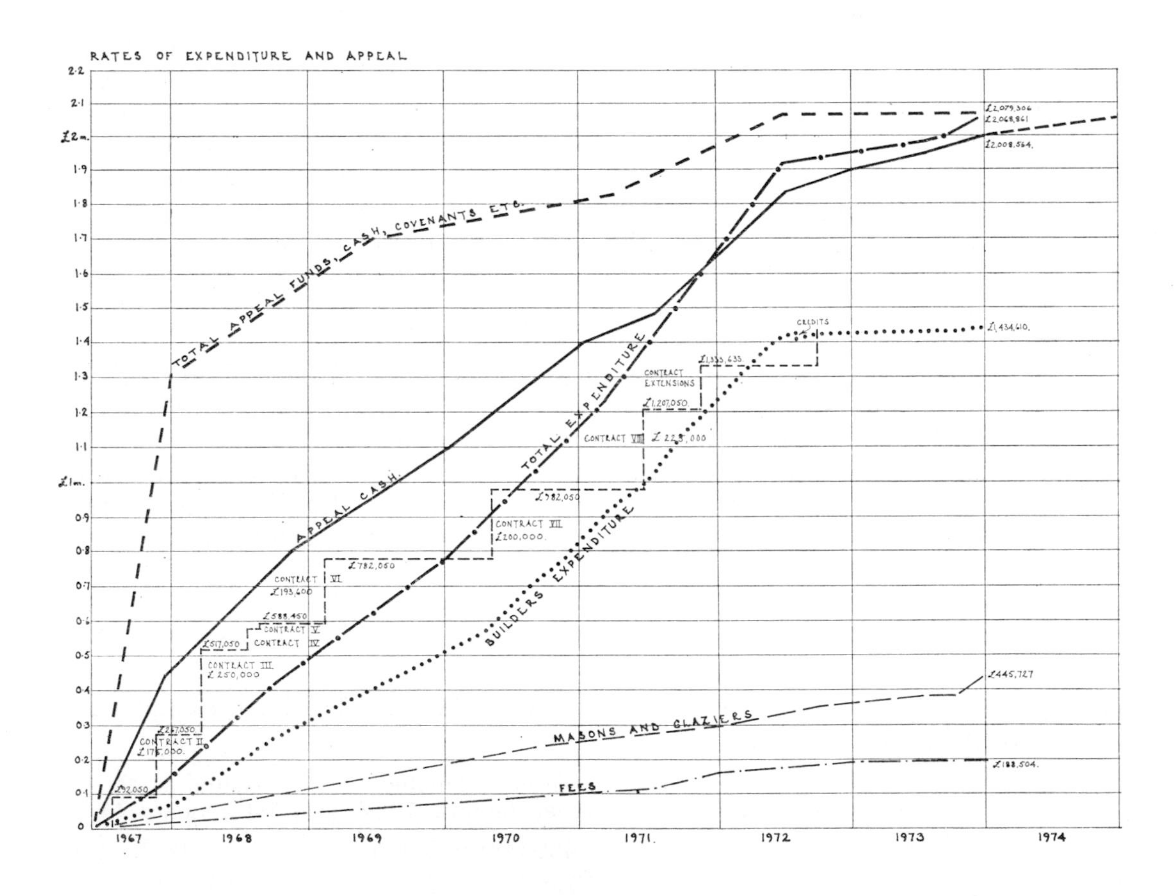

CHAPTER ELEVEN

THE CONSERVATION TEAM AT WORK

NORMAN ROSS, the resident engineer at the Minster for the last three and a half years gives one aspect of the Conservation Team at work in a short article on "Archaeology and the Engineer", and with his permission I have reproduced this almost in full.

"The indications are that, like it or not, engineers and certainly building contractors are going to have to pay far more heed to the claims of archaeology than they have to date. As a nation we have, on the whole, been irresponsible in the way that we have abused sites of historical importance for no other reason than economic expediency. The blame lies not primarily with developers and contractors but rather with local and national government, and even, as will be discussed later, with antiquarians themselves. As far as the building industry is concerned, the reasons for this irresponsibility are the common ones of ignorance, indifference, and a lack of guidance from those who should know better, i.e., architects, engineers and the planning authorities. We can start to make amends by educating ourselves.

"Archaeology is defined by Professor V. G. Childe in his book *A Short Introduction to Archaeology*. He begins, "Archaeology is a source of history, not just a humble auxiliary discipline. Archaeological data are historical documents in their own right, not mere illustrations of written texts. Just as much as any other historian, an archaeologist studies and tries to reconstruct the process that has created the human world in which we live—and us ourselves in so far as we are each creatures of our age and social environment. Archaeological data are all changes in the material world resulting from human action or, more succinctly, the fossilized results of human behaviour. The sum total of these constitute what may be called the archaeological record."

"This record is therefore a material record of soil layers, pottery, walls, floors, graves, etc., and is unique to any one site. To destroy it before it has been properly recorded would be rather like burning an ancient manuscript before reading and photostating it. In each case we would lose forever one fragment of communication with the past.

"Moreover the archaeological source of history of any particular site might be the one and only source. Those of us involved with the restoration work at York Minster have been made aware of one archaeological 'problem period'—the Dark Ages, which span the 5th to 9th Centuries A.D. Any area that is known to have been inhabited in pre-Norman times could be of vital importance to us. The history of the York Minster site begins in the Roman era but the strata being most diligently excavated are those which form the post-Roman occupation levels.

"Once we have appreciated the importance and relevance of archaeology we must come to an understanding of the techniques which an archaeologist uses to extract the maximum amount of information he can from a site. It is the sense of incomprehension which leads to feelings of frustration in a contractor as he watches an archaeologist at work. What is the man doing? Why is he excavating with a trowel in layers only 5 mm. thick?

"The only thing that an archaeologist and a contractor have in common is the removal of soil. The methods differ because the aims differ. Archaeology, in essence, is the removal of deposits in the reverse order of their deposition. If any deposit leaves slender evidence, careful investigation is called for.

"Contrary to common belief, the study of ancient structures or monuments in itself is not the primary function of an archaeologist. It is the history of the structure that interests him, and its history is contained in the layers of soil which surround and cover it. If the occupants of the building were very houseproud, the layer of deposits left by them might be very thin and contain very little evidence of habitation such as potsherds, coins, and metalware. The archaeologist depends heavily on such artifacts for dating the period of occupation and consequently would wish to dig very slowly and carefully. On the other hand a deposit might be fairly thick, perhaps even several feet, and could be dealt with more quickly. Examples include areas of demolition and thick layers of silt deposited during extended periods of flooding. If, for one reason or another, time is against him, the archaeologist must make a value judgement about the time he spends on any particular area or level of the site. Ideally, of course, such a situation would never arise.

"It is fascinating to watch an archaeologist at work. What appears at first sight to be nothing more than a pile of builder's rubble is immediately classified by the archaeologist as a 'feature'. Careful scraping with a trowel (sometimes a spatula and paintbrush) reveals it to be a Roman wall or a Saxon fireplace or even a group of tightly-packed graves each with ornately-carved slabs and headstones. In association with the Roman wall there might be an area of opus signinum floor of crushed red tile and mortar which would be painstakingly cleaned and recorded; or possibly some slabs of painted plaster which at one time would have decorated a room. Where it is possible, all finds are preserved and conserved for exhibition either on site or in a museum.

"Archaeologists prefer to excavate a site in a manner which enables them to see the whole site at once and simplifies the photography and surveying which is a very important aspect of their work. Consequently they can leave high soil sections around the perimeter of their dig, useful to them as references, but which raise the whole question of safety.

"In the past, archaeologists have relied on their own common sense in this matter, receiving professional advice when the site falls within the domain of a city engineer's department or similar body. Unfortunately commonsense occasionally takes second place to stronger emotions and over-zealousness has led to tragic endings. On the site of York's city wall, not 300 yards from the Minster, a Royal Commission archaeologist was killed when a 15 foot high trench collapsed and buried him. He was taking a calculated risk with the pressures of time and money against him which makes his death even more needless and adds to the pertinence of this article.

"The subject of safety is one of many which bring us as engineers into the field of archaeology. We can give advice, for example, on matters like surveying techniques and mechanical means of soil disposal. We can offer opinions on structural problems. Is an arch within a foundation there as a relieving arch or for another purpose altogether? Did these twelfth century foundations ever carry a substantial load? The benefits of a close relationship are, of course, mutual, since the engineer or the contractor could receive valuable advice during the site investigation stage resulting in reduced costs. But perhaps most important of all we can help the archaeologists to organise themselves efficiently and to plan the best way of dealing with a particular site.

"At present there are two possible methods for providing for archaeology on any development site. One is to allow for it within the contractor's programme of work. In other words the site remains the total responsibility of the contractor from the start of the contract, and archaeological activity is permitted only within a set period and under terms set out in the contract. The other method is to hand over the site initially to the archaeologists for research, either until they have finished or for an agreed duration, after which the contractor takes possession.

YORK MINSTER ARCHAEOLOGY

"At York Minster the situation has slowly evolved, after a struggle, into something approaching the former method. The site is said by some to be the most important in this country. It is certainly one of the most important, situated as it is in the centre of the Roman fortress of Eboracum—the capital of Brittannia Inferior; the Roman 'Whitehall'; after the departure of the legions, a religious and political centre with great European standing. Under the floor slabs of the Minster lies part of the principia, possibly the commandant's house, Saxon remains, and parts of the huge Norman cathedral.

"When it was first realised that something was drastically wrong with the foundations of the central tower, an initial inspection of part of the substructure was carried out under the guise of an archaeological dig. As soon as the contract for the restoration work was signed, however, archaeology came a very poor second to the need for rapid excavation. This began in a very unarchaeological manner, despite the setting up of an advisory committee under the chairmanship of Sir Mortimer Wheeler.

"The contract work at the Minster thus began with the premise that archaeology was only to function within the limitations of a watching brief. Initially, only one archaeologist was appointed on secondment for a year with a possibility of continuing to try and record as much as possible of a mountain of material; inevitably, he was forced to withdraw by the pressures of the task. Archaeology on the site has been struggling ever since to recover from that inauspicious start.

"It has been a sad situation in many ways, particularly as much of the difficulty was unnecessary. Now, with the benefit of hindsight, we can question why the difficulties arose, not in malice but in the hope of easing the path of others in the future. There seems little doubt that the main responsibility lies with the archaeological community, and in particular with the Advisory Committee, for they failed on two crucial counts.

"First by not making it sufficiently clear right from the outset to all concerned—the client, engineer, contractor and, particularly, the general public—just how important the site was historically. The client, in the form of the Dean and Chapter of York together with the trustees of the appeal fund, thus were not made to comprehend fully and to acknowledge that the site must contain an invaluable record of early British history. In fact the client tended to play down the fact that archaeologists were present, apparently in the mistaken belief that this was in the best interests of the project.

"For our own part we ought to have insisted more strongly than we did on a sequence of excavation to give as much time as possible for archaeological research. Regular, precise measurements are taken of the movements of the fabric. These give an indication of what Bernard Feilden calls the patient's temperature. Together with visual inspection and sound judgement the measurements enable us to be in control of the situation and to advise on the safe limits for excavation.

"The contractor must also be included in any list of culprits. He deserves some sympathy as he has probably suffered financially as a result of the general shortsightedness. However, whilst admitting that he received inadequate instructions, he could and should have been more understanding of the difficulties facing the archaeologists. He could have been much more flexible in his methods of excavation and shoring. We all might also have made better efforts to try and interest his workmen in antiquities. One of his labourers might then have experienced a feeling of dismay when the point of his pneumatic drill pierced an exquisitely carved Northumbrian hogback tombstone!

"By no means all has been lost. The publications which will follow the completion of the work will be eagerly received by historians all over the world. The Saxon church has not been found, as had been hoped; but the findings include an extensive Saxon graveyard on an alignment parallel with the axis of the Roman fortress which runs north-east to south-west. This circumstantial evidence has led to a concensus of opinion that the Saxon foundations were not simply incorporated into the Norman work. Much has been learned or confirmed about the Roman buildings and the Norman cathedral. In addition, archaeology has demonstrated that it is a source of history by the discovery that, in the thirteenth century, York Minster had two twin projecting towers adjoining the eleventh century Norman west front, a fact not previously known or even suspected. A very large number of artifacts have been extracted, among them some of the finest Saxon tombstones in this country. Another valuable find was a large quantity of painted Roman plaster, once a wall decoration, showing scenes from life 1600 years ago. Part of the plaster has already been assembled like a giaantic jigsaw into a panel measuring eight metres long by 3.4 metres high. It is displayed in the Undercroft formed around the new foundations. The preserver is Dr. Norman Davey, a retired civil engineer!

"What are the lessons we can learn from the experience of York Minster? There is patently a need for much better communication. If a site is archaeologically important, let the fact be stated unequivocally by all interested parties, in particular by the antiquarians. Let the Government take steps to ensure that everyone is informed and let Parliament legislate, as others have, to ensure that the claims of archaeology are not brushed aside. Sufficient funds must be forthcoming to deal fully with the research. If they do not come from private resources then the Government must provide them. Let there be an adequate team of professional archaeologists who are engaged full-time on a proper contract basis with a brief to study and record a site in as short a time as is practicable and to publish their report. The team should receive advice from the professions concerned with building and the backing of experts in fields like soil analysis and conservation. They should be able either to hire their own plant and labour, or to have it seconded to them by the contractor. The ramifications of insurance, compliance with building regulations, etc., should be worked out thoroughly so as to avoid a situation where there could be divided responsibilities.

"It is time that we all awakened to the danger of being described by future generations as barbarians. In this conservation-minded decade we must make every effort to preserve our heritage and our history.

"In conclusion, I should like to acknowledge the assistance given in the preparation of this article by Derek Phillips, Director of Archaeology at York Minster."

Norman Ross' criticisms may seem hard, and I accept some share of them for not understanding enough about the significance or the problems of the archaeologist. Now with our joint experience on York Minster we must try to pass on information to our successors. The scale of the job and time pressures must be remembered but with the benefit of hindsight I would have insisted upon the following, if I had a similar task once again.

(1) A team of about twenty expert diggers with a professional, as opposed to an amateur, approach to the logistics of their task.

(2) A survey grid based upon a system of ten foot squares for use by both engineer and archaeologists.

(3) Forecasts of what the dig would be likely to find. For example, we could have been told that we would be likely to find Roman walls upstanding more than five feet, or be given a diagram of the alignment of these walls. This information turned out to have a vital significance in the special arrangements of the undercroft museum but was never considered in our appraisal of the foundation design. Luckily the right decision was made purely on grounds of being better engineering.

Of course the prime difficulty was financial. As the Dean said, "How can we spend money upon an archaeologist who is a civil servant, when it is being collected from the parishes of Yorkshire. They don't want to pay a civil servant's salary." In fact, only £7,500 of appeal money was spent upon archaeology, as in due course the Ministry of Works (now Department of the Environment) made large grants, and further grants came from the British Academy, the Pilgrim Trust and the Wolfson Foundation. The total cost of the dig was £59,000 over some six years. This appears costly; but about twice as much should have been budgeted from the beginning. Yet to have done so might have been an overall economy in avoiding difficulties for the contractor and adjustments to the programme.

Trying to do things cheaply is often the most expensive way; yet, in fact, the archaeologist's information was vital for the correct solution to the problems of the Minster. Their slow and careful digging was also a safety precaution in one sense. Their record photographs helped me, as surveyor, monitor many aspects of the work without having to be present all the time. Our enhanced understanding of the Minster's structural history enabled the team to omit structural works which, upon reappraisal with the help of archaeological information, were found to be no longer necessary. Perhaps the most dramatic example of our collaboration was when we were about to build 45 feet of concrete wall, Derek Phillips said, 'Why not prod and see if there is not a Norman wall there?" I asked the builders to prod and, rather as in a Biblical miracle, after about five prods the earth fell away and there was a magnificent wall which is now to be seen in the undercroft under the north transept.

There were, of course, inevitable conflicts. Ken Stephens' role was to manage and programme the job. He had the healthy instincts of a contractor to use a bulldozer if anything was liable to stop him doing his proper job, and with this I could sympathise. Archaeology is impossible to forecast or programme, and archaeologists are not trained as architects are to make value judgements of imponderables. This I had to do sometimes, so that no blame for some archaeological bloomer fell upon the overworked Derek. Nevertheless, to destroy knowledge of the past wantonly is an unforgiveable sin. I found that by making Ken and Derek expose both sides of the problems in my hearing, if I let the matter simmer for the rest of the day they often came with a joint solution to me for final approval. Each respected the integrity of the other; and I imagine Derek will concede that he has learned a lot about safety precautions, job management and the concept of programming from the others on the Minster job and, in particular, from both Ken Stephens and George Preston.

I have dealt with the archaeologist's problems at some length because they were acute. The engineer's problems were obviously most important; and here I must say that after our joint experience on York Minster, I don't recognise the difference between engineers and architects. We were all involved together, and I found that the best man somehow volunteered the solution to each problem. The engineers were really marvellous and brought a quality of understanding and depth of knowledge that was in my experience unique. Poul Beckmann modestly wrote, "Our work at York Minster is not an intellectual 'tour de force' nor will it be spectacular when it is finished, but it is nevertheless engineering. What makes it particularly interesting is that the problems are four dimensional. Time enters into the technical arguments very much and we cannot begin to understand what has happened to the structure without studying its history."[1]

David Dowrick joined the team as project engineer about a year after the start, coming straight from the Sidney Opera House. He showed great zest in climbing about the scaffold without the help of proper boarding and delved deep into the archaeological problems, even coming up from London to work on a Sunday, when they were hard pressed. At the end of the job he got engaged to the sister of Norman Lister the project architect. Was this symbolic of our joint attitude to architecture and engineering?

Dare I say it, but I think the thinking of the engineers changed considerably due to this exposure to history. It also now seems less positivist and more willing to consider analogy.

However, the first rule for anyone considering restoring an ancient structure is how to make best use of the material there. One can argue that the building has stood for five hundred years in spite of the calculations, and by conserving the existing fabric and augmenting it one must be able to make it a bit better. One can also exploit the inherent synergy of the structure. Synergy is the phenomenon that the strength of the whole is greater than the sum of the strength of the parts; or put otherwise, a building gets the habit of staying up.

The team were supported by the benevolent attitude of Sir Ove Arup and his partner Geoffrey Wood, and a large number of staff in London—in particular Andrew Lord, the soil mechanics specialist, whose contribution of scientific knowledge was most important.

1. York Minster and its problem (p. 3).

Richard Jennings was assisted by Peter Turner in designing and supervising the heating installation. Churches present difficult problems with regard to down draughts; and the heating consultants advised on a series of hot air jets to form a blanket of air at triforium level. They also advised additional perimeter heating and the provision of conditioned air to the choir in order to protect the organ and wood work against desiccation. The height of the tower was exploited by using a high pressure hot water system which had higher operating temperatures and therefore can economise on pipe sizing. New 35 sec. oil-fired boilers were installed so as to reduce the sulphate content of the fuel that was burned; and a new properly sized chimney, lined with fire brick and cased with stone, was built by the Minster masons in 1968.

John Sinclair, who had worked with me previously, was the first electrical consultant but he decided to emigrate to Australia. He was succeeded by Charles Eaves, whom I hope will continue to serve the Minster for many years. The electrical consultant had one of the hardest jobs—without the possibility of a firm brief, without working drawings, and having only a rather larger than life building to work upon. But until the engineering work was defined, he could have little idea of a possible programme; and it was obvious that the brunt of the last six months would fall on his shoulders. With the addition of "Son et Lumière" in the programme, the special acoustic problems of sound reinforcement and then the lighting of the undercroft, his cup was more than full of work.

Lastly the quantity surveying work was done by Frank Hall and Martin Needler, who inherited my own approximate estimates which I have set out previously on pages 51-2.

Frank's role was cost controller, and it was made explicit that he had the authority to veto any proposal on cost grounds. Cost control on a project such as this is even more vital than an ordinary job, for charitable appeals have no reserves to draw upon should costings go wrong. We therefore had to be very careful to work within agreed budgets and not to start work that could not be finished. Priorities therefore had to be put in the right order. Yet once committed to a project, it had to be done properly, and all other works that might be done economically at the same time should be included. A lot of these items could not be foreseen, but they tended to add up in cost. Also inevitably and inexorably the cost of the main works tended to increase, partly due to their inherent difficulties and partly due to inflation, for which I had not allowed specifically in my first budget.

Frank Hall attended the Appeal Fund trustees meetings and spoke independently of me as cost controller. I thought it best for a Yorkshireman to be answerable to Yorkshiremen on this important matter. I think we have few regrets about the matter of allocation of funds, inevitably we made some small mistakes; but we got the big decisions right, particularly with regard to continuing with the work to the western tower foundations, which were taken in our stride but might have cost more than half again as much if done later.

The professional team and the appeal administration costs were extremely low. All professionals were paid on an agreed time basis, thus giving great flexibility with regard to allocation of work, each of us in a sense taking in some of the others washing in the interests of overall efficiency. Professional barriers were therefore dissolved and we all worked together.

Lastly, work on a project such as this has to be true team work. The team spirit emanated downwards from the Dean and High Steward; and it is in this context that my partners gave a dinner after the special Builders' Festival Service on April 28th 1972 for all the men who had worked on the Minster for over a year. Here Lord Halifax, the second High Steward, announced that a large gift received that day had brought the appeal fund to its target of £2 million.

Then the Dean gave Mr. Peter Shepherd, on behalf of all the men who had worked on the Minster, a silver and gold gilt goblet depicting the works of craftsmen, which was a tribute to their work.

CHAPTER TWELVE

THE FUTURE

BESIDES the roofs and lead coverings what is there left to do? There is a vast amount of stonework which needs restoration. Pinnacles, string courses, weatherings, gargoyles and buttresses—all need urgent attention. My opinion is that there is work for the twelve masons in the Minster Stoneyard for the foreseeable future and beyond. The stoneyard itself has been improved and mechanised by the purchase of compressed air tools and a new diamond saw, and equipped with new rust proof galvanised scaffolding and hydraulic props. The Minster masons can do Gothic restoration work second to none in this country. Recent examples of their work can be seen in the doorway from the nave leading into the new bookshop.

Programming to date has been dictated by the urgency of the foundation work; and the masons have had to work here, there and everywhere on the Minster during the last five years. It is now hoped to programme the work so that they can carry out their task of restoring the equivalent of five bays of the nave aisle each year. If this programme can be carried out, it should be possible to get once round the Minster in 30 years; and then it will be necessary to start again, because caring for the Minster is a never-ending task. This programme is illustrated in the plan overleaf.

When people ask, "How long will the Minster last?" The simple answer is that it will last as long as it is wanted, now that the fundamental problems of the foundations have been resolved. One can only show that it is wanted by caring for it and maintaining the fabric against the ravages of wind, weather and pollution; but it should be stressed that in financial terms the problem of the restoration of the masonry in the superstructure will add up over the years to a sum as large as that spent upon the foundations.

In a book such as this it is not possible to show all the intricate details which have gone into the restoration work; but a large number of illustrations have been provided and are set out in the order of the work, and captioned fully so as to enable a fuller understanding of what was achieved in restoring the Minster. For architectural and engineering specialists the report of Poul Beckmann and David Dowrick on the structural work is included as an appendix.

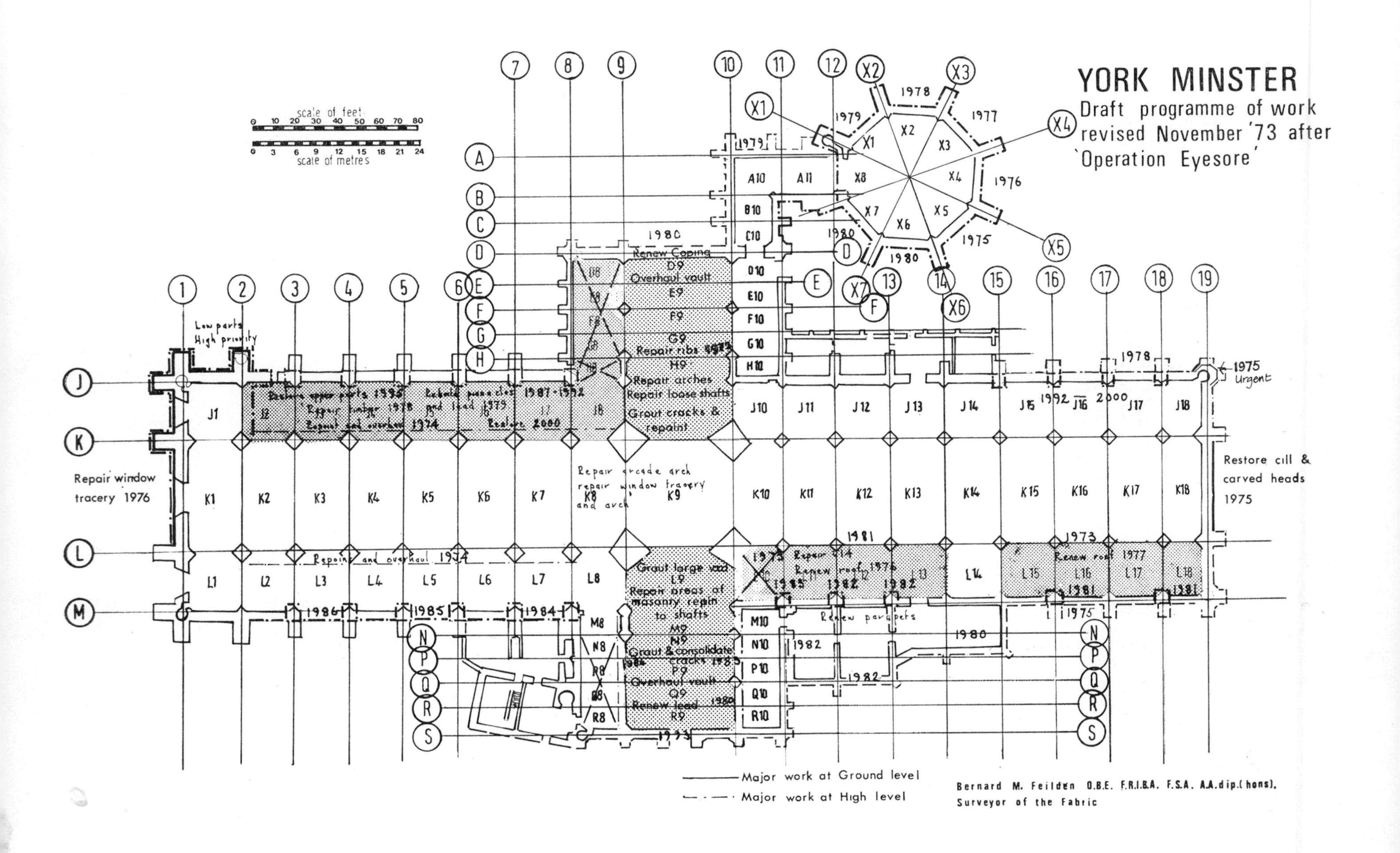
YORK MINSTER
Draft programme of work revised November '73 after 'Operation Eyesore'
scale of feet
scale of metres
Low parts High priority
Repair window tracery 1976
Restore cill & carved heads 1975
1975 Urgent
Renew Coping
Overhaul vault
Repair arches
Repair loose shafts
Grout cracks & repaint
Repair arcade arch repair window tracery and arch
Grout large void
Repair areas of masonry repair to shafts
Grout & consolidate cracks
Overhaul vault
Renew lead
Repair and overhaul 1974
Renew parapets
Renew roof 1976
Renew roof 1977
Restore 2000
Major work at Ground level
Major work at High level
Bernard M. Feilden O.B.E. F.R.I.B.A. F.S.A. A.A.dip.(hons).
Surveyor of the Fabric

APPENDIX A

Service for the Northern
Province and Northern Cities
York Minster
St. Peter's Day Thanksgiving
29th June, 1972

Sermon by the Archbishop of York (Dr. F. D. Coggan)

St. Matthew, 16. 15, 16. "You", Jesus asked, "Who do you say I am?" Simon Peter answered "You are the Messiah, the Son of the living God".

My mind goes back to the day, some five years ago, when Lord Scarbrough sat in my study at Bishopthorpe. I asked him if he would become the first High Steward of York Minster. He was, as many here will remember, a quiet, humble, self-effacing man. But he was also a man of quick decision and of strong determination. At once and with no questions he acceded to my request. Then we faced together the task of restoration that had to be undertaken, though, at that stage, we were not fully aware of its gravity or its magnitude. I shall never forget what he said to me: "I don't believe in writing letters. I believe in going to people in person." So he did. Having climbed up to the triforium and clambered over curved vaults, having seen the desperate danger in which the old Minster was, he went out personally to canvass his friends and make them his allies in a great cause. It is very largely due to his vision, his tenacity of purpose, his untiring personal effort, and his inspiring leadership that success has crowned the efforts of the Dean and Chapter, of the architect and his team, which we celebrate today.

It was three years ago today that Lord Scarbrough died. How fitting it is—and for me how high a privilege—that I should dedicate, as I intend to do in a few moments, a memorial to him under the tower for whose restoration he was so largely responsible; and that we should sing together the hymn which was his favourite and which was sung at his Memorial service—"God is working His purpose out as year succeeds to year". We salute his memory, and we say to his loved ones: "We are grateful for what he did and, above all, for what he was".

We—you and I and the host of friends near and far who came to the rescue—tackled the task of restoration only just in time. It was 500 years ago this month that this building was re-dedicated after the completion of the series of rebuildings which had gone on almost continuously since shortly after the Norman Conquest. What Archbishop de Grey envisaged in 1215 was completed during the Archbishopric of George Neville, when Richard Andrew was Dean in 1472. But 500 years is a long time, and the pillars had grown tired of carrying the great weight of that central tower and the foundations had given way. Mercifully science had reached that point in its evolution when its skills could effect a sure rescue operation—and effect it they did.

These great buildings—our Minster, St. Paul's, the Abbey—*matter*. These great national shrines speak to men of the things that are eternal, and bear witness to the Christian presence at the heart of our national life. They help us to see ourselves in a proper perspective. If anyone of us cherish any delusions about his own importance, let him stand for five minutes before the high altar, one frail mortal in the midst of *all this*, and he will soon get his sense of proportion right. We do well to preserve these buildings and to beautify them.

What an extraordinary combination of skills has gone to the achieving of this restoration! Architects and archaeologists, historians and artists, scientists and financiers, craftsmen and technicians—all have had their share in preserving for future generations one of the most magnificent buildings in Europe. Generous donors—corporations and business firms, wealthy individuals and old age pensioners, organisations and little children—have clubbed together to raise the largest sum ever previously asked for in this country for the restoration of a church. We are here to thank God for that—and we do, from the bottom of our hearts.

But I would ask you to let me share with you a concern which has long been on my mind. Let me put it this way. We Englishmen and women are the heirs of a long Christian tradition. That tradition has profoundly affected our laws, out education, our art, our music, our architecture, our whole way of life. We all realise that, some very clearly, some more dimly. So, when anything which embodies that tradition is in danger—when, for example this Minster is in peril of collapse—we are prepared, and rightly so, to dig deep into our pockets and ensure its safety. That is good. But let us not think that that is Christianity, for it is not. Christianity is not a nod of approval, nor a subscription, nor a cheque however generous. It is something which cuts much nearer the quick than that; something infinitely more demanding and more personal. It has to do with a man's response of mind and will to the God who has gone out to him in Christ and who would meet him face to face.

We gather today in a Church which bears the name of St. Peter. The Gospel appointed for his day describes a scene of great interest. As I read it, I can picture the scene. Here is a small crowd of men, engaged in heated discussion. There had irrupted into their midst a young Man who had made a tremendous stir in their society—everybody was talking about Him. Sitting loose to convention, His presence and teaching were uncomfortably new. Jesus challenged old ideas, and faced men with new ones, and there was about Him a freshness and a purity which somehow made them feel shabby. Now He interrupted their debate. "What are people saying about Me?", He asked them. A perfect flood of answers came back, some pretty flattering; they even compared Him with some of the Old Testament giants. Then he faced them; and those clear eyes looked disconcertingly straightly into their own. "You", He asked, "who do you say I am?" The chattering ceased. The interesting discussion ended. They saw it, with a kind of blinding clarity, that religion was not an intellectual interest in historical figures or in antiquarian affairs. It consisted in facing up to a Person and His demands. One man dared to answer. It was Simon Peter. "You are the Messiah", he said, "the Son of the living God." What's *that*? A bit of theoretical theology? On no! Far from it. That was a personal response to a personal confrontation—and it altered his whole life. If *that* was true, if God had indeed broken in—in the Person of Christ, if the young Man who faced Peter was in fact the Son of the living God, life could never be the same again. Mind and heart and will, his whole life-pattern, were affected. Peter must be Christ's bond-man to the end of the journey.

And so it proved. The fisherman became the courageous Christian leader, the pioneer, the daring innovator, the martyr, all because of that meeting with Christ, that confession of the truth. *That* was religion.

That *is* religion—so intimately personal that no one else, not even your nearest and dearest, can make the response for you. So demanding, that you are thrown back on the grace of God that comes to you, fresh every day, in prayer and communion. So closely impinging on every activity that you find you must avail yourself of the resources, provided within the Christian community, of sacrament and preached word and bracing fellowship. *That* is religion. Not an interest in the trappings, but an obedience to the Son of the living God.

That is what the Minster is *for*. That is what the Dean and Chapter long that it should increasingly become—a House of God where people in need, like you and me, find Christ to be to them the Way, the Truth, the Life itself. If it is not that, it is a very beautiful but a hollow historical monument. If it is that—as indeed it will be more and more—it will be none other than the house of God, it will be the gate of heaven.

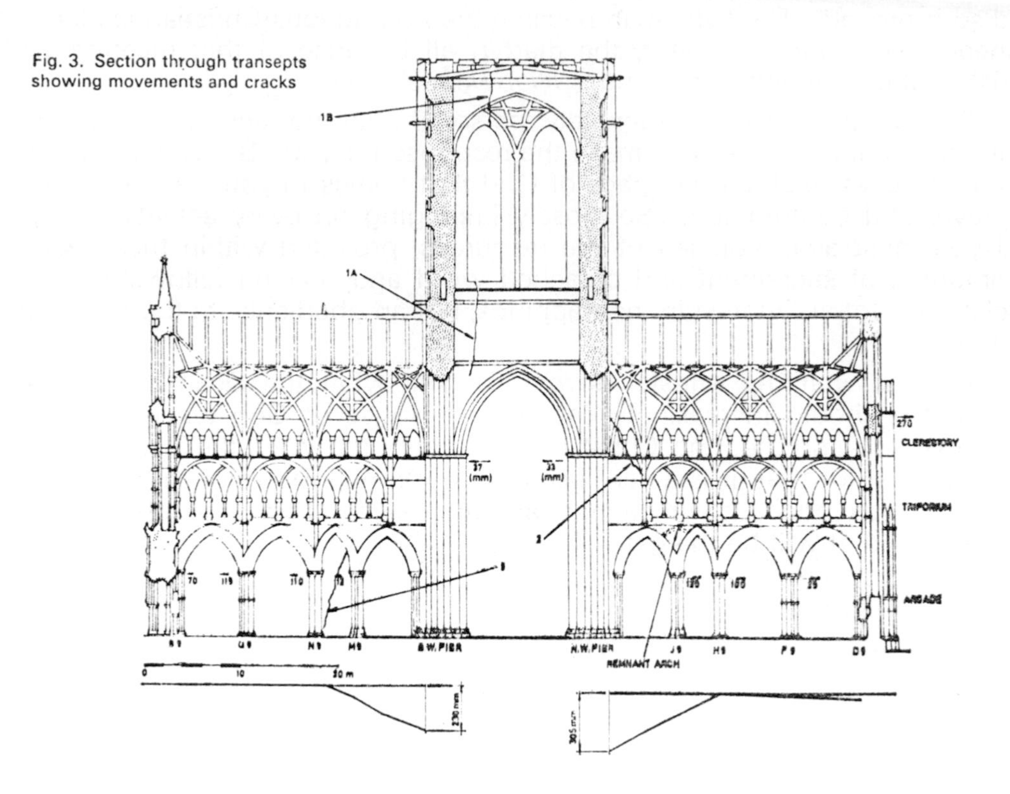

Fig. 3. Section through transepts showing movements and cracks

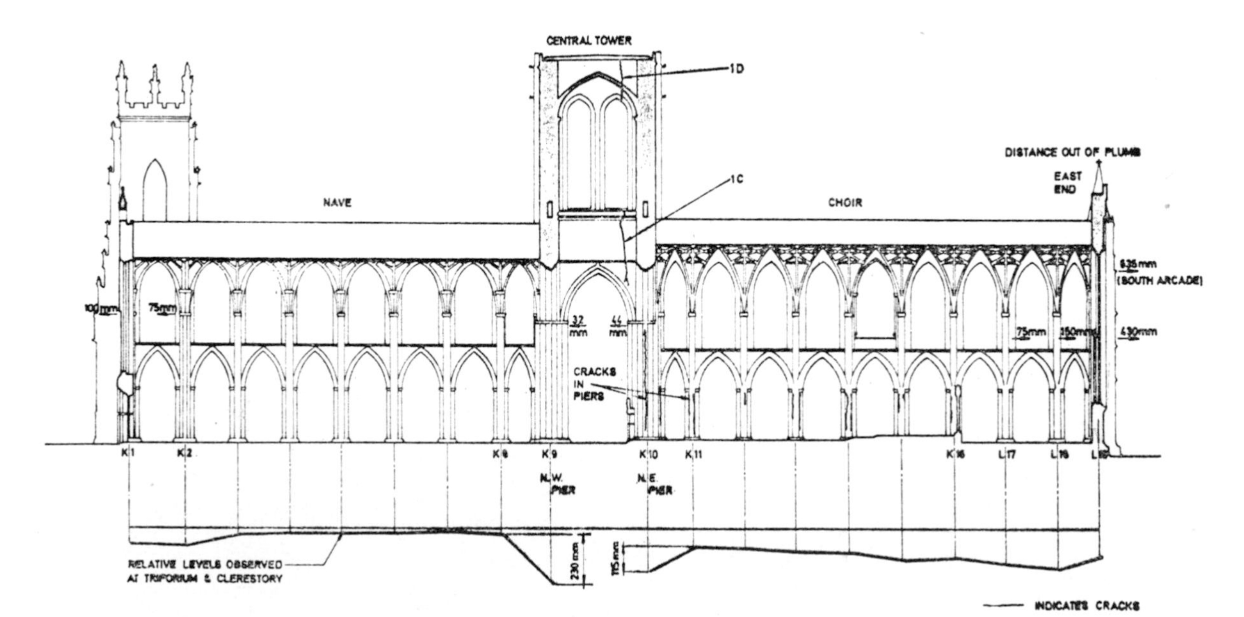

Fig. 4. Section through nave and choir showing movements and cracks

APPENDIX B

THIS APPENDIX contains extracts from the paper 'York Minster structural restoration' presented by D. J. Dowrick, BE, MICE, MNZIE and P. Beckmann, MSc, MICE, MIngF of Ove Arup and Partners who gave the above paper to the Institution of Civil Engineers on 21st December, 1971 (Paper 7415 S).[1] They were subsequently awarded the Telford Gold Medal for the paper. The abbreviated paper describes methods employed in quantifying the structural defects brought to light by the inspection of the Surveyor to the Fabric in 1966. The methods and results of the site investigation are outlined. An account is given of the structural analyses of the central tower superstructure and the foundation calculations which together indicate differential settlement, mainly due to overloading of the ground, as being the main cause of the observed structural damage. The design of remedial works to the central tower, includes a reinforced concrete ringbeam at roof level, 46 stainless steel rods placed in holes 21 m long drilled in the thickness of the walls below the lancet windows, and reinforced concrete extension footings connected to the existing masonry foundations by prestressing. The long term stability of the east end wall is shown to have been suspect and the strengthening of the great east window by horizontally draped wire ropes is described, as is the design of the underpinning on the wall. Finally a description of the steel shoring to the east end with its constant pressure jacking system precedes an account of the movements recorded during the execution of the works. The extensive engineering works at the west end of the Minster are not discussed in this paper, but are similar in principle to those in the central tower.

Structural analysis of the central tower area

49. Various structural analyses were carried out to help determine the causes of the cracks and other deformations, the overall stability of this part of the structure, and what remedial works might be required.

50. There were considerable difficulties in determining the gravity loads with satisfactory accuracy, due to the scarcity of reliable drawings. In view of the excessive time, cost and the physical difficulty of carrying out a full geometric survey, the masonry volumes were measured from the nineteenth century architectural drawings supplemented with check measurements on leading dimensions, particularly wall thicknesses. The masonry density was assumed to be 2400 k/gm^3. The vertical load on each of the four main piers of the central tower was found to be about 38 MN while the normal arcade columns in nave and choir carried about 3 MN.

Methods of analyses for the superstructure

51. At the beginning of the investigation there was no recognised, comprehensive method for determining stresses, deformations or stability of a masonry structure as complex as the section through the lantern and transepts Fig. 3 shows.

52. Some early attempts at simulating the tower structure by an equivalent lattice frame foundered on the difficulty in allocating suitable stiffnesses to members representing panels of masonry.

53. Two analytical techniques proved useful in the end. The first used as its mathematical model a rigid frame of thin members, enclosing shear panels where appropriate to simulate the effect of masonry panels. The calculations, including finite element analysis of stresses in the shear panels, were carried out with the aid of a digital computer. The second method was graphical thrust line analysis. The two methods were found to complement each other, each yielding information on different aspects of the structural behaviour of the fabric.

Frame analyses

54. The first frame which was analysed, represented a north-south section through the tower and the transepts. Two load cases were considered: gravity loads, and in plane differential settlement of the tower as a whole relative to the transepts. When comparing the calculated deflexions (Fig. 16) with the observed it became clear that the outward sway of the transepts could not have been caused by gravity loads from the present tower, nor by its settlement. In the first case the central tower piers should have leant outwards substantially, which they did not, in the second case there was complete disparity between calculated and observed movements.

55. This discovery seemed to create an impasse which was only resolved when one of the historians relayed the information from one of the mediaeval documents that at the time of the

1. Paragraph numbers and references to illustrations have been retained from the original report.

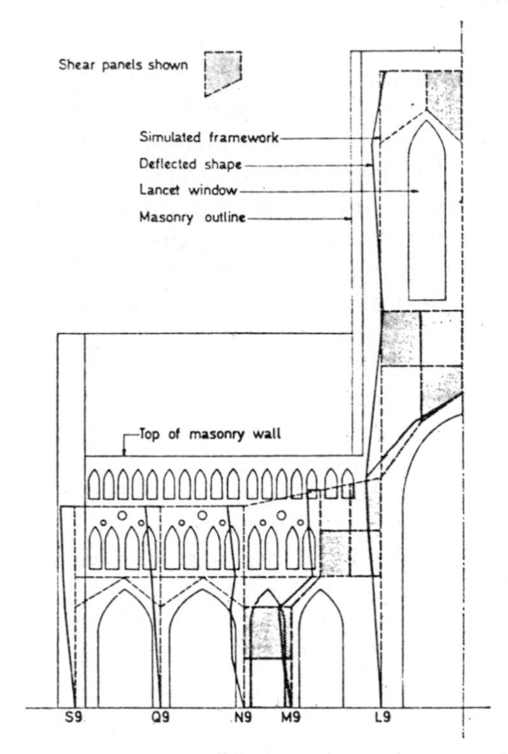

Fig. 16. Calculated deflexions of central tower and transept due to gravity loads acting on an uncracked simulated structure (cf. Fig. 3)

construction of the present transepts in the thirteenth century a central tower had been built, which had partially collapsed in 1407 and subsequently had been replaced by the present lantern. It was the thrust from this early English tower which caused the lateral movement and explained the discrepancy between theoretical and observed calculations.

56. The calculations also indicated that relative settlement of the present tower would produce high diagonal tensile stresses in the infill panels between the close spaced transept piers (H9-J9, H10-J10, M9-N9 and M10-N10 in Fig. 2), but only one of these panels was cracked, namely M9-N9. This was explained by examination of the masonry features which indicated that only M9-N9 had been filled in prior to the building of the present tower—the remaining three having been added in the eighteenth century, leaving sufficient time for the primary settlement of the new tower to be complete.

57. In order to ascertain the effect on the calculated stresses of using a closer mesh of frame members and shear panels a repeat analysis was carried out on just the tower using the same load cases as for the first frame. It was found that for examination of overall behaviour a fairly coarse mesh was adequate.

58. As the previous analyses had assumed the masonry to be uncracked, and in view of the size of some of the lantern cracks it was decided to study the effect of these cracks on the stress flow, as well as the interaction of the central tower with the nave and choir arcades which although much larger than the transepts were more lightly built. An east-west section through the central tower was therefore represented by the third frame in which the large crack in the north face of the lantern was allowed for by deleting some of the shear panels beneath the window as shown in Fig. 17. This was not strictly correct as the frame was assumed symmetrical implying a similar crack under the other window, left of the centreline, but this simplification did not prevent a reasonable evaluation of the general effect of this crack.

59. Figure 17 shows the thrust lines derived from the gravity load case. It is apparent that the main thrusts readily adjust to the cracking without significantly affecting the overall stress flow. Unlike in the transept frame, most of the horizontal thrust from the lantern arches is absorbed by the main pier itself. Once again, however, the gravity load thrust lines lie comfortably within the masonry.

60. The main result from the differential settlement load case was the calculated reaction of the bay adjacent to the main pier. The lack of any deep shear panel in that bay resulted in less load sharing by the adjacent piers. In fact the measured levels indicated that virtually no vertical load had been transferred across the arches of this bay, as the adjacent choir or nave piers had not settled with the central tower (Fig. 4). Unlike those in the transepts these arches were too short in span to accept the differential settlement without unsightly failure (Fig. 6).

61. From the work already done it could be seen that the cracks in the lantern were probably

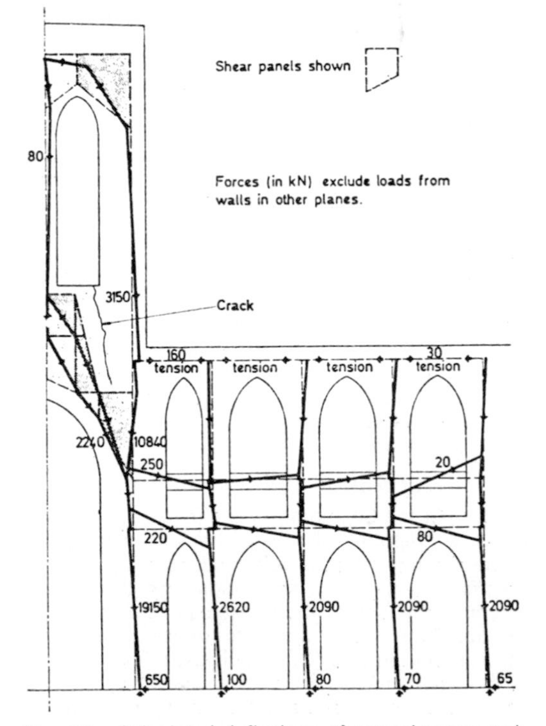

Fig. 17. Calculated deflexions of central tower and choir (or nave) due to gravity loads acting on a simulated structure incorporating an existing crack

due to differential settlement of the central tower, but not just a simple settlement of the central tower with respect to the surrounding structure. There was evidence that the north-west pier had settled more than the other three main piers of the central tower, and further levels were now taken on the four corners of the central tower, at four positions, namely the pier springing points, the capitals, the lantern gallery and the roof. A clear pattern emerged as can be seen in Fig. 18(a) indicating that the north-west pier had settled

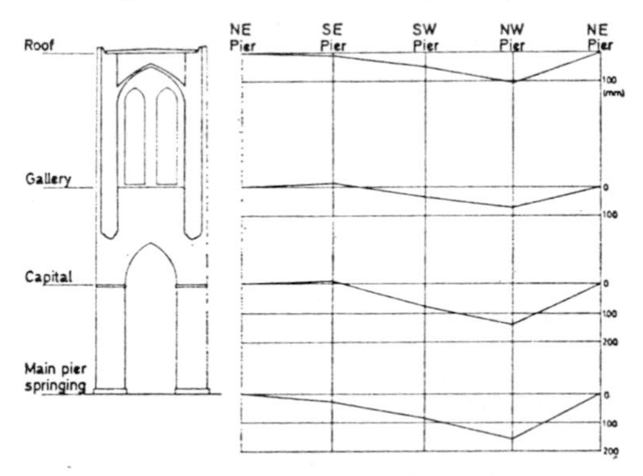

Fig. 18(a). Differential levels of the four corners of the central tower measured at various heights

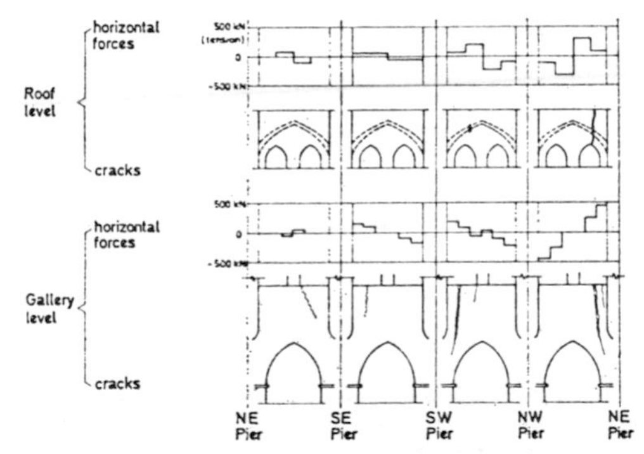

Fig. 18(b). Observed cracks and horizontal forces calculated assuming the differential settlements shown in Fig. 18(a)

75 mm relative to the others during the period of construction and had settled a further 50 mm after completion of the gallery. The south-west pier seemed also to have settled relative to the north-east and south-east piers.

62. To investigate the effects of such settlements on the lantern a three-dimensional framework with shear panels was set up (Fig. 19), and a unit vertical deflexion was applied to one corner. As the frame was symmetrical the effect of any size of settlement at any corner could then be obtained easily by appropriate superposition and combination of the computer output. A brief study of the results indicated horizontal tension below and above some of the lantern windows. Assuming that the north-west pier had settled 1.0 units and the south-west pier 0.5 units, the tensile forces above and below the windows were plotted and compared with the crack pattern (Fig. 18(b)). The major cracks corresponded exactly with zones of high tension, and although the smaller cracks did not match so well this was not really to be expected in ancient masonry of variable strength.

63. As for the cracks above the lantern windows, these also corresponded in position to the highest horizontal tensions indicated for this differential settlement pattern. It was therefore concluded that the cracks in the lantern had been caused by the main piers settling differentially to each other, the principal effect being due to excessive movement of the north-west pier.

Graphical thrust line analysis

64. Whereas the foregoing analyses had been helpful in establishing the causes of various cracks and the effect of differential settlement, graphical thrust line analyses were carried out principally to determine the present overall stability of the central tower, and a credible position for the centre of thrust at the base of the main piers for use in foundation calculations.

65. The graphical analysis assumed that all arches were three-pinned, and the pin positions were arbitrarily chosen generally to mobilize minimal horizontal forces. This choice took account of possible arch spread, and was also compatible with the actual crack positions although these had in fact occurred for other reasons. The computation was independent of any assumptions regarding tensile strength of

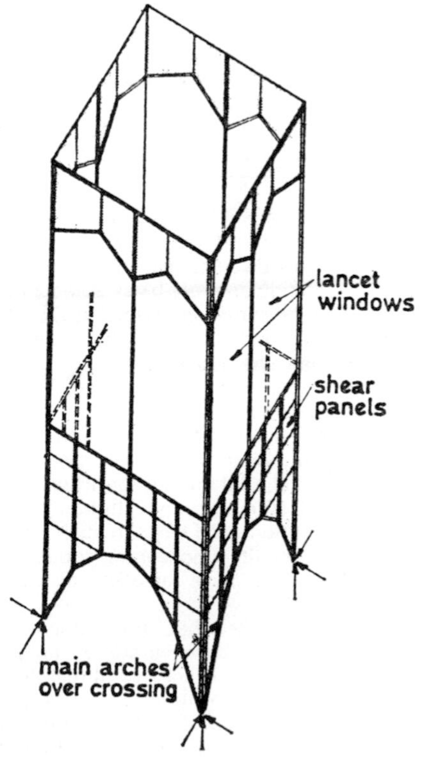

Fig. 19 Three-dimensional framework simulating the central tower lantern for assessing the effects of differential settlement

masonry, and because cracks could be easily taken account of, the graphical method was probably more realistic concerning overall stability than other methods. In addition, it was simple, quick and explicit.

66. Two load cases were studied, gravity loads and wind in the east-west direction, each with varying amounts of buttressing from the nave or choir arches. Fig. 20(a) shows a resulting thrust line, which satisfies the basic requirement that the thrust line should always be a safe distance within

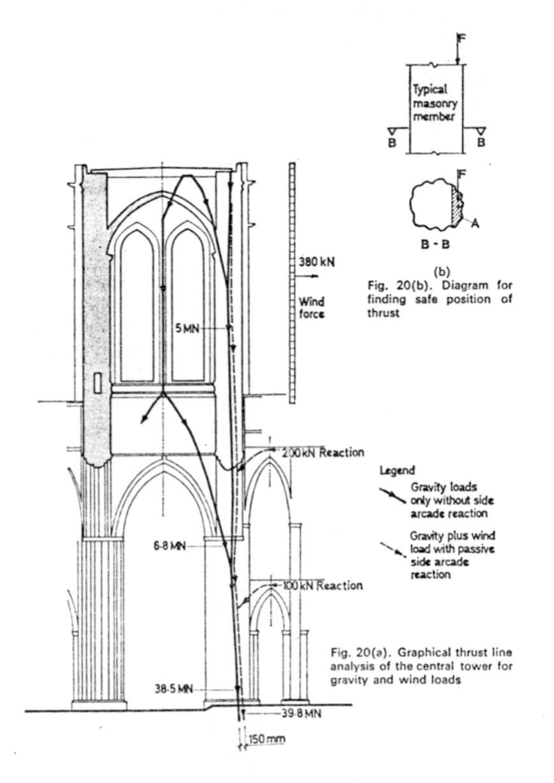

(b)
Fig. 20(b). Diagram for finding safe position of thrust

Fig. 20(a). Graphical thrust line analysis of the central tower for gravity and wind loads

the masonry. This distance may be computed by assuming a rectangular stress block symmetrically disposed about the thrust line (Fig. 20(b)). If the thrust (P) divided by the areas of the stress block (A) is less than the crushing strength of the masonry, then the position of the thrust line at that point is realistic and safe.

67. The thrust lines indicated that the central tower main piers would have stood safely under gravity loads alone, without any buttressing from the surrounding structure, and although it may not have survived full wind loads in such a condition comparatively little horizontal support was necessary from the nave arcades to achieve stability.

68. It should be noted that as the structure had been made statically determinate by arbitrarily chosen pin positions, the lines of thrust formed would not necessarily be the actual ones, but as equilibrium had been satisfied the solution was statically admissible, as discussed by Heyman.[2] While the actual position of the thrust line may not be necessary for the stability criteria under the assumptions of plasticity, some of the stress computations of the soil required a reasonably accurate thrust position in order to be meaningful. It was estimated that with a sensible choice of the arch pin positions and considering the size of the main piers, the actual thrust position at floor level would be within about half a metre of that calculated, and that this order of accuracy would be satisfactory.

The safety of the existing tower substructure

69. As the Norman footings had been badly bent and cracked by the four main piers, not all the existing footing area was effective in transmitting the pier loads to the ground. The actual effective areas were considered to be those enclosed by the truncated cones fanning out from the pier pedestals at an angle of 45° to the vertical, corresponding to the shear cracks. For the north-west pier the effective area was 85 m^2 upon which was imposed a total vertical load of 45.3 MN giving an average bearing pressure of 530 kN/m^2. According to the thrust line calculation this load was applied with an eccentricity of about 1 m, for which allowance was made by the methods of Meyerhof and Brinch Hansen which both modify the eccentrically loaded area to an equivalent smaller uniformly loaded area. After Meyerhof the average bearing pressure was 720 kN/m^2, and after Brinch Hansen it was 750 k/Nm^2.

70. According to Brinch Hansen the ultimate bearing capacity was 800 k/Nm^2 for the eccentric load. This figure was however an underestimate as it assumed $\phi = 0$ for the subsoil, whereas part of the failure zone would in fact pass through the boulder clay which generally had some internal friction.

71. The multi-stage triaxial tests on the boulder clay had shown $\phi = 13.5°$, but no definite value for the internal friction had emerged. Nevertheless, an attempt was made to gain an indication of its effect. Assuming values of $\phi = 5°$ and $\phi = 10°$ for the whole of the soil mass affected, ultimate bearing capacities of 1030 kN/m^2 and 1380 kN/m^2 respectively were obtained, producing corresponding factors of safety of 1.3 and 1.8.

72. The geometric simplifications of the footing layout made in the calculations and the assumptions of zero shear transfer across the shear cracks in the footings, meant that the calculated safety factors were conservative. But the actual safety factor was nevertheless uncomfortably low as was quite evident from the deformations of the footings.

Settlement calculations

73. As most of the structural damage to the fabric in the central tower area appeared to be the result of differential settlements of the main piers, it was necessary to have a full understanding of the past settlements and present tendencies. Calculations of the settlement caused by the construction of the present central tower were made, using consolidation data from laboratory tests on the soil samples.

74. Based on the average consolidation test results, the four main piers were calculated to have settled about 380 mm whereas midway between the main piers the settlement should have been

about 110 mm. This theoretical difference in level corresponded to what had been found on the actual structure, and hence gave some confidence in the assumptions on which the calculations were based.

75. As mentioned earlier the north-west pier appeared to have settled more than the other three main piers, although equally loaded. The consolidation data from the borehole immediately beside this pier seemed different from the others. A settlement calculation based solely on these results indicated a main pier settlement of 490 mm, and a possible differential settlement of 110 mm of the north-west pier compared to the other main piers. This again was of the same order as the corresponding measurements on the actual structure. The differential settlements observed in the central tower area were therefore feasible in terms of different compressibilities of the subsoil alone, without there necessarily having been other contributory factors.

76. The primary settlements quoted in §75 represent the bulk of the total settlement, and from the coefficients of consolidation it was estimated that these settlements would have taken place over a period of about 65 years. Although the comparatively slow rate of construction would have affected the duration of settlement somewhat, the primary settlement must have been largely complete by the early sixteenth century.

77. Secondary consolidation which would have occurred between then and 1970 was estimated, and it was found that the main piers probably had settled a further 90 mm while the north-west pier could have settled as much as 135 mm in that time.

78. The present day result of the differential settlements showed in the levels taken throughout the Minster at pier bases and capitals, at lantern gallery and roof and in all the triforia and clerestories. As the present fabric incorporates parts of Norman, Early English *and* Perpendicular structures which each in turn have suffered varying amounts of settlement, it was desirable for a better understanding of the effects of the settlements, to try and reconstruct the sequence of settlements. Fig. 21 shows an attempt at this in

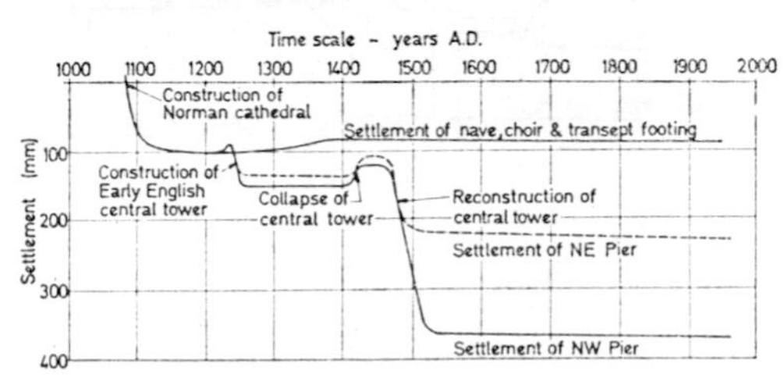

Fig. 21. Hypothetical reconstruction of settlements since 1080 AD

which the settlements of the Norman and Early English structures were calculated on the basis of their likely size and shape and an interpretation of the consolidation properties of the clay. While produced mainly as an aid to thought, the diagram nevertheless shows computed differential settlements which correspond remarkably well with the observed differences in level.

79. Future settlements which might take place under the present stress regime would clearly be much smaller than the secondary movement which had already occurred, as secondary consolidation probably decreases exponentially. Even adding the effects of drastic future lowering of the water tables, the total future differential settlements of the main piers would probably not exceed about 40 mm, which is substantially less than that which has already occurred. However, as the water tables were considered unlikely to fall significantly it was probable that the main piers would settle only about 30 mm in the future, and that the future differential settlement of the north-west pier with respect of the other three piers was unlikely to exceed 10 mm.

Design of remedial works to the central tower

80. Three separate strengthening projects were undertaken in the central tower area. The two in the superstructure were to ensure that no further movement would take place in the vertical cracks in the lantern caused by the differential settlement of the north-west pier. The foundation strengthening on the other hand was to provide an acceptable margin of safety against collapse of the central tower through overloading of the clay underneath the badly deformed substructure, and to reduce the rate of any possible future settlement to a value comparable to that for the nave and choir.

81. As the cause of the lean on the transept piers, i.e. the thrust from the Early English tower, had been removed, and as it could be shown that there was no further tendency for movement, no remedial works were considered necessary in the transepts other than routine repairs of masonry.

The lantern girdle

82. The first design was that of a strengthening below the lantern windows in the region of the cracks shown in Fig. 3 and Fig. 18(b). This work was referred to as the girdle. It was necessary to provide horizontal tensile reinforcement to control the cracks. It was proposed that this should be done invisibly by inserting the reinforcement in holes drilled in the thickness of the walls. Fig. 22 shows the arrangement of twelve stainless steel bars in each wall providing a total ultimate tensile strength of about 700 kN. At normal working stresses this steel would be capable of taking all the tensile load generated by a further 25 mm of differential settlement of the north-west tower pier as calculated, assuming zero tensile strength of the masonry; and it was considered that the bars would provide adequate crack control well beyond this situation. The bars were threaded along their full length to increase their bond strength, and were to be grouted in.

83. Stainless steel was chosen to ensure a durability of the repair appropriate to the needs of a historic monument, and the strongest available alloy was specified to minimise the number and sizes of holes to be drilled. At that time the best available precipitation hardened steel was manufactured by Firth-Vickers under their designation FV 520 B which was over-aged in a temperature

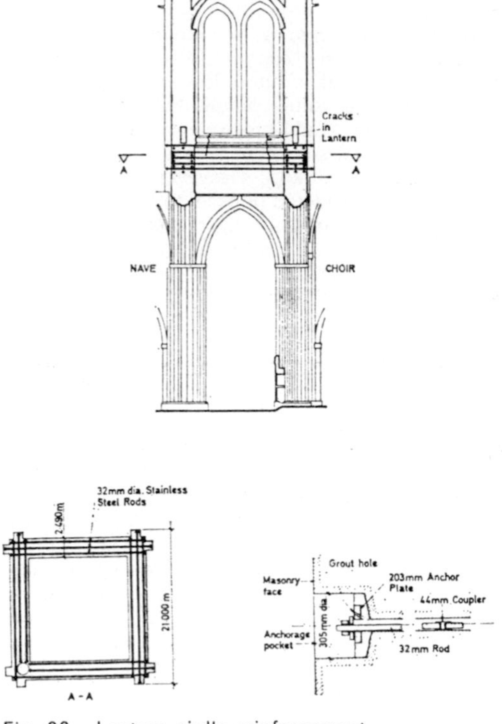

Fig. 22. Lantern girdle reinforcement

of 550°C for 2 h. A guaranteed minimum 0.1% proof stress of 800 MN m^2 was accepted for the 32 mm dia. bars used on the project.

84. Mainly because of the uncertainties of obtaining adequate bond through grout injected into ancient masonry the bars were securely anchored at the ends, in a deep pocket to allow the insertion of a stone pellet to hide the anchorage (Fig. 22).

The lantern roof ring beam

85. The second strengthening project was to provide against vertical cracks right at the top of the lantern (1B in Fig. 3). Fortunately here it was possible to make the reinforcement invisible without the difficulty of drilling through the walls. A simple reinforced concrete ring beam was provided on top of the walls during the restoration of the lantern roof which had proved necessary due to beetle attack on the original timber. Sufficient reinforcement was provided to give about 3.5 MN of horizontal tensile resistance at ultimate load.

The foundation strengthening

86. The main objective of this was roughly to double the existing bearing capacity of the foundations. In the process it would also be necessary either to eliminate or stabilise the existing badly fractured masonry substructure. The essential requirement of any chosen strengthening method was that there should be minimal disturbance to the existing load bearing structure during its execution.

87. The underpinning of masonry columns carrying 38 MN could clearly not be undertaken lightly, particularly as there was a complete lack of really comparable experience to draw from. At an early stage in the exploratory excavations a number of commercial underpinning schemes were therefore studied, ranging from complete replacement of the existing substructure with a spread footing, to various schemes using piles. As a more complete picture of the subsoil and the existing substructure emerged objections against all of these methods arose, including danger from physical disruption of the existing footings, mutilation of the lower visible portions of the main piers, and an impracticable number of piles.

88. When the extent and geometry of the existing footings had been ascertained and the clay immediately underlying the footings had been found to be reasonably firm it seemed logical simply to add to the effective bearing area of the existing foundations, if a method could be found which would simultaneously encase and stabilise the Norman substructure while causing it a minimum of disturbance in the process.

89. The essence of the chosen method was to add concrete to each side of the existing footings, drill horizontal holes through the resulting composite footing, insert prestressing tendons in these ducts and stress the whole together. Four preliminary schemes using these principles were studied, the one giving the best final structure being finally chosen although it involved diagonal and therefore potentially more difficult drilling than some of the other proposals. Figs. 23-25 illustrate the final design for strengthening the foundations

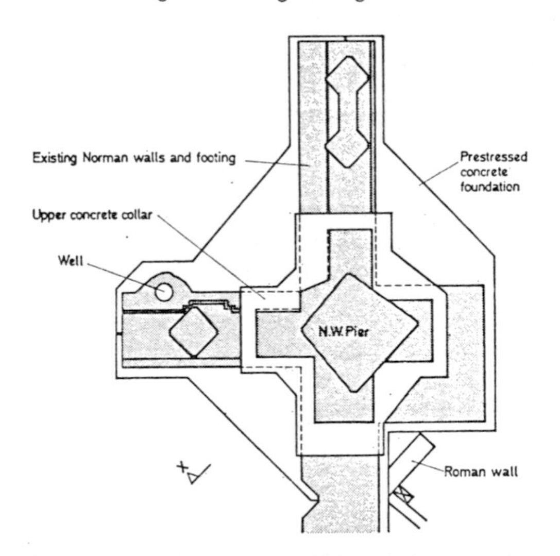

Fig. 23. Plan of north-west pier foundations showing new concrete and existing masonry

of the north-west pier. The other three main piers under the central tower were treated similarly.

90. The upper concrete collar completely encased the badly fractured remnants of the Norman walls, and was intended to distribute some of the vertical load out to the new concrete enveloping the Norman foundations.

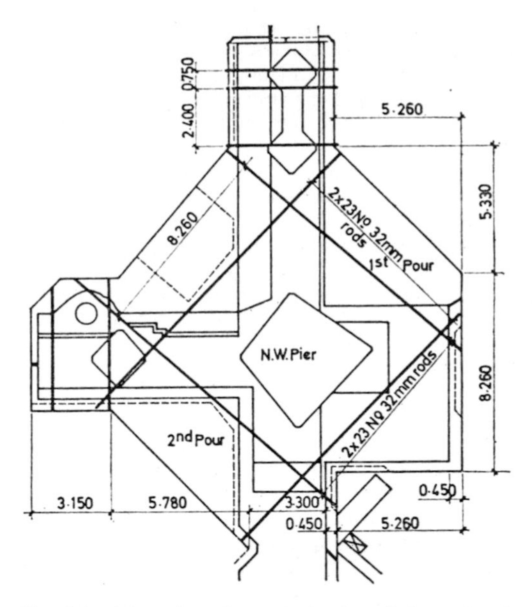

Fig. 24. Plan of north-west pier foundations showing stainless steel post-tensioning layout

91. The main blocks of new concrete were to be cast in two layers: a lower 0.6 m thick, nominally reinforced, compression pad and the upper 2.1 m thick prestressed block. The two layers were separated by a gap in which hydraulic flat-jacks were accommodated in inverted concrete troughs. After the prestressing of the main foundations the flat-jacks were to be inflated to transfer part of the pier load to the new foundation by precompressing the underlying clay. Because the total foundation area required for the main pier encroached on the adjacent nave and transept piers the latter were included in the general layout. The overall plan dimensions of the composite footing were about 14.5 m square, which reduced the bearing pressure to about 290 kN/m² and gave a final safety factor of about 3.2 compared with the calculated existing one of 1.3.

92. In order to ensure maximum durability of the prestressing tendons especially where they passed through the masonry, stainless steel rods and fittings were specified of the same material as used in the lantern girdle. The rods were however not continuously threaded, and the anchorage detail was simpler. The maximum length of rod that could be readily manufactured was 5.5 m and in certain places it was necessary to use shorter rods because of the limited clearance for insertion into the ducts.

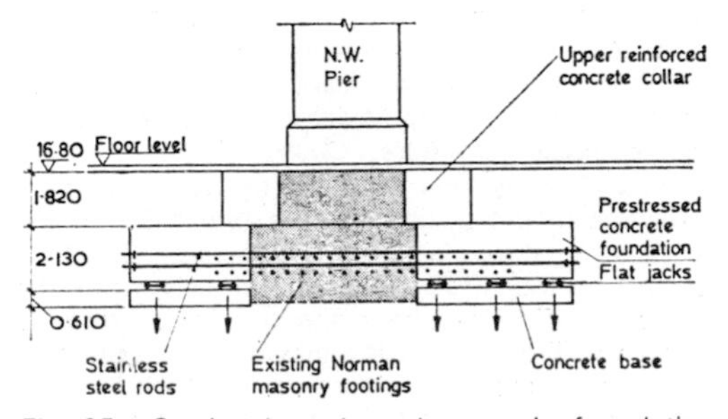

Fig. 25. Section through north-west pier foundation

93. An initial prestress of 540 MN/m² equal to 67% of the 0.1% proof stress was specified.

94. The stress levels in the foundations were low consistent with the masonry structure above, and the prestress was applied mainly to help stabilise the old footings and mobilise enough shear between the concrete and the masonry. The average compression in the new 2.1 m deep concrete due to the prestress was 0.86 MN/m².

Losses in prestress

147. The stainless steel prestressing bars in the central tower foundations were tensioned with a Macalloy Mk 10 jack which was provided with a special adaptor to fit the 1¼ in. UNC thread on the bars. The stressing operations were orthodox and simple in themselves but there was no way of predicting the losses of prestress due to compressibility of the masonry and there were no basic relaxation data available for the bars.

148. Each bar was initially tensioned to 350 kN and all bars were restressed between two and four weeks later to the same force. The losses recorded after a month varied from a negligible value to 30 kN and averaged about 15 kN or 4.5% of the initial prestress. This low figure was no doubt attributable to the low level of prestress applied to the foundations: 0.86 MN/m², and the comparatively low stress in the tendons, for although the effective stress in the threaded portions of the rods was 67% of the 0.1% proof stress, the stress level was only 55% of the proof stress over the unthreaded length of the rods.

The east end problems

Deformations, cracks and movements

98. The most striking feature of the initial measurements was that the southern buttress on the east wall had an outwards slope of 0.635 m in a height of 25 m (Fig. 4). It was not obvious how far the wall had moved during construction and to what extent it had rotated outwards after its completion.

99. A number of vertical cracks in the eastern-most bay strongly suggested that the east wall had rotated outwards since its construction, but as some differential settlement had occurred in this region the cause of the cracks was not certain. Apparently ancient cracks could distinctly be seen inside under the eastern-most aisle window, but on the outside of the building there was no trace of these cracks higher up the building. If such cracks had existed they had been repaired and weathering of the ashlar disguised the repair.

100. Inside the building, repairs, dust and lack of access again made crack detection very difficult, but close inspection above and below the triforium eventually revealed evidence of considerable horizontal elongation of the end bay. In the ceiling of the south triforium gallery there was a total width of 0.30 m of cracks and gaps in the end bay which corresponded exactly to the total

elongation resulting at that level if the outward lean had occurred after construction. There was, for example, a cleverly contrived repair of a crack, totalling 0.20 m in width. This crack had been repaired on at least three separate occasions, and contained two separate stone inserts and a mortar layer. One of the stone inserts was 0.125 m wide indicating that the crack may well have been allowed to open up that amount at one stage before being 'repaired'. The other repairs to this crack were known to have been carried out in 1830 and in 1936, and showed 35 mm of movement since 1830 and 10 mm since 1936.

101. Further evidence that the wall had been continuously moving outwards was found at the junction of the south choir aisle roof with the east wall, with signs of separation between the purlin and its seating, of about 65 mm since this roof was renewed in the eighteenth century. Similar signs of movement were found at the junction of the main roof with the top of the east wall where the ridge purlin, which was replaced in 1830 after the great fire, showed a movement of about 90 mm in 140 years. A more recent repair to the flashing at the same level showed about 20 mm of movement since 1940. These figures were consistent with those of the same date mentioned in § 100 being about twice the magnitude at twice the height showing continuing rotation of the east wall as solid body about its base.

102. As elsewhere in the Minster, mechanical strain gauge readings on major cracks were instituted at an early stage. Two cracks in the triforium were observed with great attention as these would be the most sensitive indicators of outward movement of the east wall. The strain gauge measurements were much more sensitive than any other form of measurement, but there was nevertheless a danger that the particular cracks being measured would not be live at that time. Two optical plumbing targets were therefore set up inside the east wall on either side of the great east window, and read against scales set in the floor.

103. The difficulty with interpreting any of these readings lay in the order of movement to be observed. If the triforium had moved outwards about 0.43 m more or less steadily since 1361 when it was built, then the annual average movement was about 0.7 mm, and there would be cyclical seasonal movement of uncertain magnitude superimposed upon this.

104. Regular visual inspections were made by masons and sundry professional personnel, and any signs of movement were related to the trend of the measurements and vice versa.

The condition of the great east window

105. The great east window, constructed in the years 1405-1408 is one of the biggest and most beautiful expanses of stained glass in the world. It measures 23 m high by 9.5 m wide, with its two principal mullions 0.57 m deep and the remainder 0.38 m deep. This fragile masonry structure was not only 0.60 m out of plumb but also bowed outwards 0.11 m in plan at mid-height. There was, furthermore, a tendency for the window to split down the middle because the whole of the east wall was hogging as shown by the levels of the weathering course at ground level, and a corresponding vertical crack on the line of symmetry both above and below the window.

106. The stability of this window was largely attributed to the stiffening effect of the gallery at half-height, which was probably acting as a shallow arch in plan despite some separation at the sides of the main window frame. The resistance against suction from westerly winds of the tracery in the upper half of the window, which was bowed horizontally and vertically, was a matter of conjecture.

The existing foundations

107. As nothing was known about the footings a small exploratory dig was made outside adjacent to the main buttress. It was discovered that there was no toe on the footings, the wall continuing practically straight down to founding level. In addition the quality of the foundation masonry was very poor. The founding level was about the same as under the central tower, but the lower 2 m of the footings consisted simply of roughly hewn stones without mortar.

108. It was clear that if the wall was still moving then the cause was almost certainly inadequate foundations.

Structural analysis

109. Unlike the situation in the central tower region, there was no need to investigate alternative mechanisms of collapse. Establishing the thrust line positions in the buttresses at the ends of the main arcades was the main analytical object, and two methods were used.

110. First the two end bays were considered as a plane framework consisting mainly of shear panels with no allowance for cracks. Gravity and wind loads were considered and the position of the thrust line in the end buttress was found to be within the middle third of the masonry in both cases.

111. Next a graphical thrust line analysis was carried out to highlight any differences between the present cracked and the original uncracked structure. Assuming three-pinned arcade arches of maximum rise the horizontal arch thrusts were found to be quite small, and the effects of wind and the outward slope of the end buttress had more influence on the position of the thrust line. The position of the thrust line at the bottom of the end buttress was found to be virtually the same using both types of analysis, so that the arcade arch thrusts were very similar in the uncracked and in the cracked structure.

112. Because the safety of the wall was very sensitive to the position of the thrust line in the buttress a further graphical analysis was done assuming increased horizontal thrusts from the arcades. The resultant thrust line diagram is shown in Fig. 31. As the maximum compressive stress in the masonry at the bottom of the buttress was small (2.5 MN m^2), it appeared that the cause

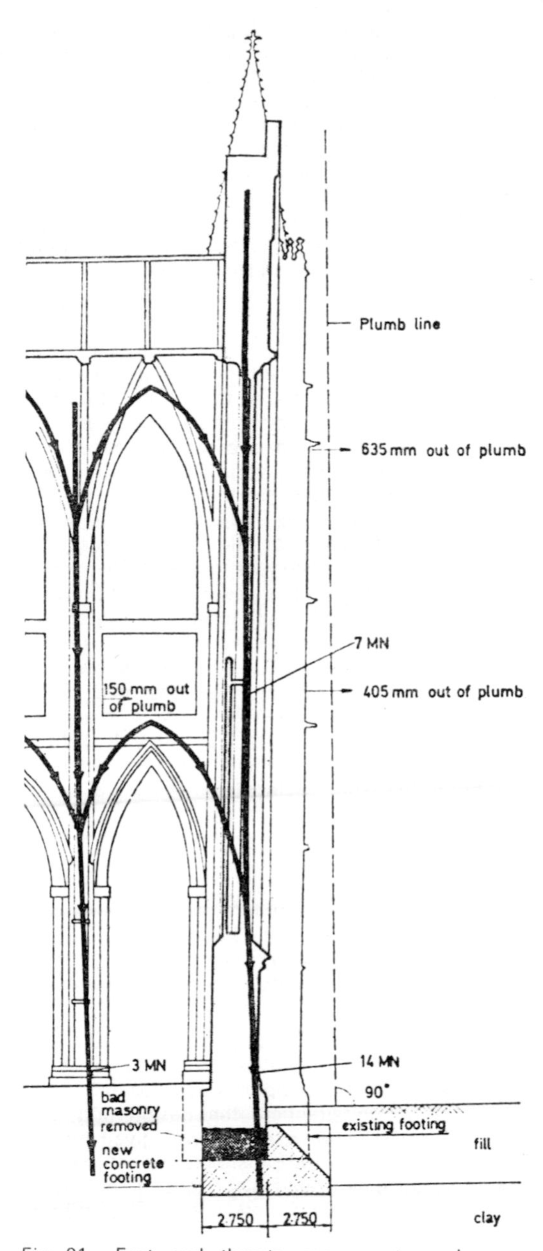

Fig. 31. East end thrusts, movements and new footings

of the lean was to be found in the foundations rather than in the superstructure.

The stability

113. A calculation was carried out to find the margin of safety against failure of the subsoil. Under the assumption that the footings were everywhere similar to those found in the exploratory dig, the existing foundations would have been as shown in Fig. 32.

114. It was clear from the crack up the centre of the east window and the slopes of the various buttresses that the east wall had acted in two separate halves. Considering the south half only, it appeared that it had acted as a rigid body in the ground underneath. Although the presence of the buttresses complicated the calculations, Brinch Hansen's method[5] was used. Allowing for some tolerance in the position of the centre of load on the foundations and also for the scatter in the shear strength of the clay, the factor of safety against failure of the clay was found to lie in the range 1.25-1.55.

115. If it were assumed that the footing in the vicinity of the main buttress next to the great east window was acting independently then the safety factor area was somewhat smaller. Either way the safety margin was not satisfactory. The clay

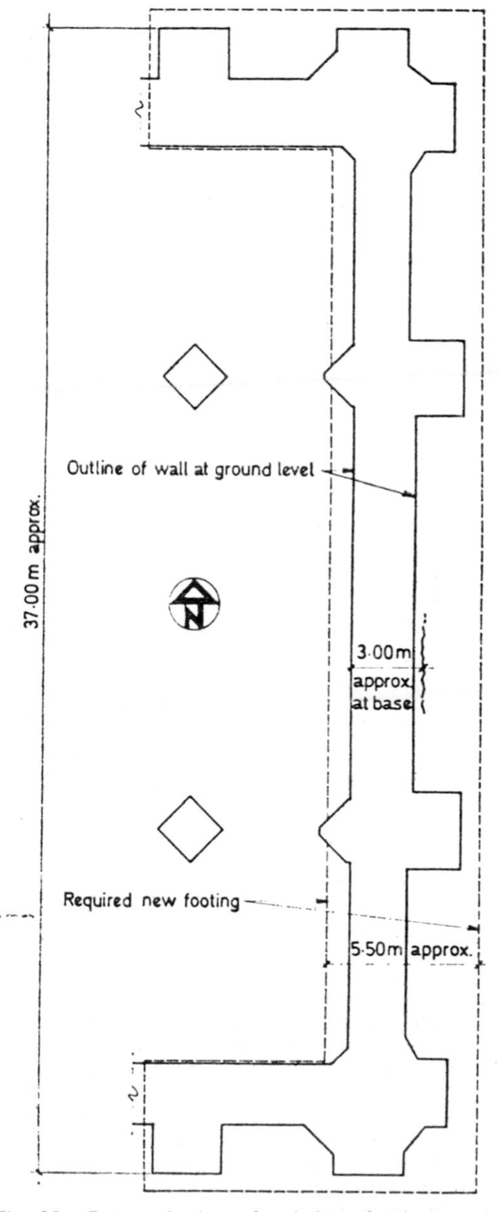

Fig. 32. East end plan of existing footings and underpinning

had yielded in the past allowing the wall to rotate outwards, and this was a continuing, progressively worsening phenomenon which would eventually end in the east wall falling outwards.

The design of remedial works at the east end

Bracing the great east window

116. It was essential to secure the great east window from eventually falling outwards. To dismantle its leaning mullions and reconstruct them in a vertical plane was not only a major building project, but would also impose the extra wear and tear of removal and re-fixing on the very fragile glass which was 560 years old. It was therefore decided to try to strengthen the window in situ, in the least conspicuous way.

117. The easiest position at which to strengthen the window was at the gallery at half height. Although this was undoubtedly acting as a flat horizontal arch, the safety margin it provided was uncertain, as it was impossible to determine the shear strength across the masonry joints, or how much arch thrust could be developed at the supports. The method of strengthening chosen for this member was to insert a horizontally draped cable as shown in Fig. 33. It was designed to withstand outward wind suction by catenary action if the masonry arch were to fail. This cable consisting of a 25 mm stainless steel wire rope could be completely hidden from view by laying it on the top surface of the gallery.

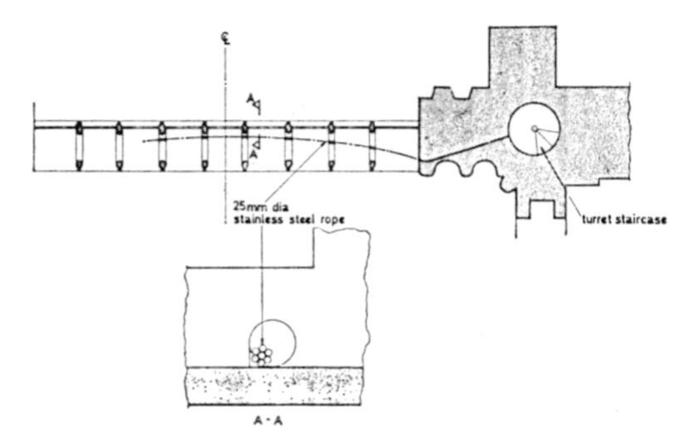

Fig. 33. Plan of great east window gallery strengthening

118. Assuming that the wind load from a 9.5 m height of the window was to be supported at gallery level the maximum tension in the cable was 100 kN compared with the breaking load of 340 kN.

119. It was not possible to estimate the horizontal deflexion under wind load because the stiffening effect of the masonry could not be predicted. However, in the worst case assuming no stiffening action by the gallery itself, and assuming that the parabolic form of the wire rope was maintained, the outward deflexion of the gallery under full wind load was calculated to be 38 mm. Even if this extreme situation could occur, the deflexion would safely be accommodated in the joints between the mullions and the glass panels over the full span of 9.5 m.

120. With the strengthened gallery the double mullion system below it was estimated to be sufficiently strong, but the upper half of the window could not be left to span vertically between gallery and window arch. It was decided to provide three further horizontal cables. These cables were designed as horizontal suspension structures and were the same size as the gallery cable. A small initial tension was applied in order to take the slack out of the cables.

121. The cables were attached to the major mullions of the tracery at carefully selected points with adjustable stainless steel anchor bolts.

Underpinning the east wall foundation

122. To prevent the east end wall from eventually falling outwards it was necessary to provide a substantial toe to the existing footings. The chosen scheme was simply to replace the existing foundation with a complete new one of twice the size (Figs. 31 and 32). With the new footing width of 5.5 m the average bearing pressure was reduced to 270 k/m² and the safety factor against failure of the clay increased to 3.40 from being possibly as low as 1.25.

123. By arranging the centre of thrust from the superstructure to be well inside the inner half (or heel) of the footing it was hoped to reverse the tendency for the wall to rotate outwards.

124. The underpinning was designed to be carried out in headings 1.22 m wide in such a sequence so as to cause the least possible disturbance to the fabric and minimal temporary increase in ground pressure. Safety against the wall rotating outwards during the works was provided by temporary steel shoring which will be described in §§ 149-152.

125. Although basically a mass concrete design, some lateral reinforcement was required in the bottom to provide for bending tension in the toe. As the total footing was concrete, ordinary mild steel was considered sufficiently durable.

East wall shoring

149. As soon as it was determined that the east wall was rotating slowly outwards and would have to be underpinned, the design and construction of temporary shoring was given priority. The design criteria for the shores were somewhat arbitrary as they would avert disaster merely by preventing continuing movement, rather than by relieving the stresses in the ground.

150. It was decided that an adequately robust design would be achieved if the two main shores were designed to withstand the arch thrusts from the choir arcade and clerestory. East-west shores were provided on each of the four buttresses on the east front and a north-south shore was used at the north-east corner because the north half of the east wall had tilted north as well as eastwards.

151. The shores were straightforward steel trusses founded on simple spread footings but incorporated a somewhat novel load-control device. This took the form of a pair of *Freyssi* flat-jacks in tandem at the base of each shore connected to a constant pressure cell. A known load was thus jacked into each shore and auto-

matically maintained throughout the underpinning. The constant pressure cell in the hydraulic circuits caused the flat-jacks to expand or contract in compensation for any temperature movements in the steel shores. If the shores had been fixed-ended the working compressive stresses in the main booms could have increased by about 40% due to seasonal expansion.

152. The constant-load facility also had the advantage of preventing over-loading of the shores as the east wall settled during the underpinning. A total movement of 50 mm at 45° to the vertical was provided by the pair of flat-jacks. This proved sufficient to cope with the temperature movements as well as the induced vertical settlement.

Settlement measurements

Measured settlement of the central tower

153. Because of the past and possible future differential settlement suffered by the fabric, it was desirable that a comprehensive long term levelling routine should be put in hand taking absolute levels on various parts of the structure. A permanent deep bench mark was sunk to bedrock in the nave and three shallower temporary bench marks were also used in other parts of the building.

154. A Vickers 577 automatic levelling instrument was used, with a plane-parallel glass plate micrometer which allowed readings to the nearest 0.2 mm.

155. The main use of the precise levelling during the works period was to monitor the effect of the underpinning on the superstructure. Mainly due to the relief of overburdening, each of the four main piers settled about 20 mm, a typical time-settlement curve being that of the north-west pier (Fig. 40(a)). The rate of settlement was accelerated by increases in the excavation rate, by cutting through the old Norman footings

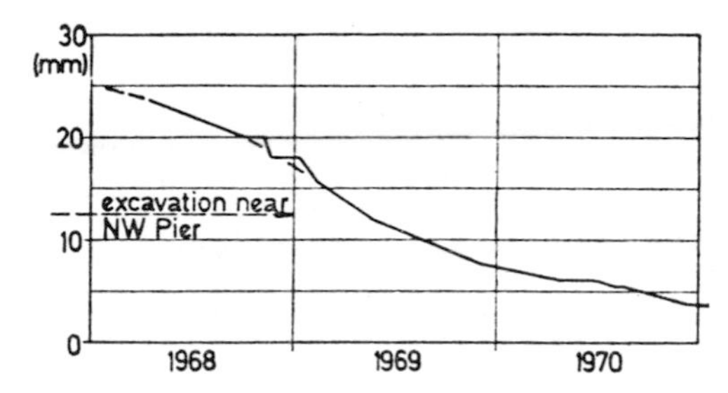

Fig. 40(a). Settlement of north-west pier induced by the excavation

and also slightly by the drilling operations. Temporary replacement of some of the overburden by sandbagging helped to minimise these settlements.

156. This degree of induced differential settlement of the main piers with respect to the neighbouring structure naturally caused fresh distortion to some of the superstructure. Some ancient shear cracks started to move again, but with remarkably little need for repair work. The main concern was to protect the stained-glass windows in the bays adjacent to the central tower. This was achieved by freeing the appropriate panes from the surrounds, leaving the window supported on the saddle bars, thus avoiding complete removal of the glass.

157. Figure 40(b) compares the differential settlement of the north-west pier and pier H9 (Fig. 3) with the corresponding movement of crack 2 also shown in Fig. 3. It is interesting how closely the two curves follow each other, especially

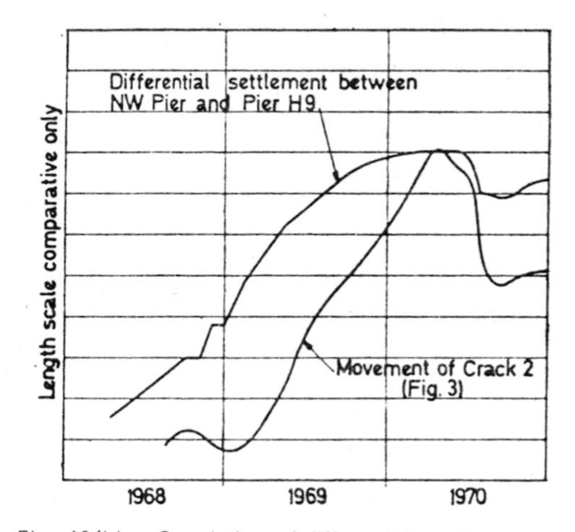

Fig. 40(b). Correlation of differential settlement and shear crack movement adjacent to the north-west pier

considering the type and magnitude of the structure and the distance between cause and effect.

Measured settlement at the east end

158. The underpinning method at the east end was a classical one of driving headings (1.22 m wide) and it was thought that by limiting the number of headings open at any one time to four and by keeping simultaneous headings well separated in plan the effects on the superstructure would be negligible. However, the amount of induced settlement was somewhat greater than anticipated due mainly to a failure during the initial site investigation to determine correctly the nature of part of the upper clay stratum.

159. What was initially believed to be sandy

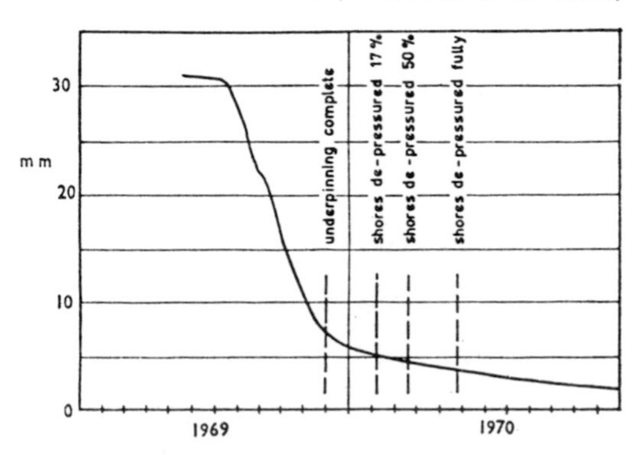

Fig. 41. Settlement of the east wall induced by the underpinning

clay was subsequently found to be clay with sand laminations in a stratum about 1 m thick. This layer was very sensitive to the excavation process, swelling considerably and rapidly upon decompression and consolidating correspondingly when loaded by the new foundation. As a consequence the resultant final induced settlement of the east wall was about 20 mm. There was however only little damage to the superstructure and the main preoccupation was the stained glass. The works were carried out as symmetrically as possible and with the minimum time lag between exposing the base of the excavation and concreting so as to minimise the effect of settlement on the great east window which emerged with only one or two minor cracks.

160. Once the settlements had slowed down sufficiently after the completion of the underpinning, flat jacks under the east wall shoring were deflated in three stages over a period of 11 weeks. Levels were taken on a total of 15 points on buttresses around the east end related to a temporary bench mark in the park opposite. A time-settlement graph of a point on the centre of the east wall is shown on Fig. 41 together with the sequence of pressure release.

Acknowledgements

161. Space does not permit individual mention of all those who through their involvement in the project have assisted the Authors. This is the more regrettable as many gave their help in an entirely unofficial capacity out of their interest in the building.

162. Those primarily concerned were The Very Rev. Alan Richardson, Dean of York; Mr. Bernard M. Feilden, Surveyor to the Fabric; Mr. K. Stephens, Area Manager and Mr. G. Preston, Contracts Manager, Shepherd Construction Ltd.; Mr. Derek Phillips, leader of the archaeological team and members of the Royal Commission on Historical Monuments (England) and particularly Mr. J. H. Harvey.

Acknowledgement to the authors and Institution of Civil Engineers for permission to reproduce over half the above paper are gratefully recorded. Some interesting points have inevitably had to be omitted but most of the omissions are covered, perhaps inadequately, in the main text.

THE MINSTER from the SOUTH WEST

Minster views from the walls

A visitor to York Minster will be well advised to walk along the ancient medieval walls to York Minster. This way he will avoid some of the worst of modern traffic and get the pleasure of approaching the Minster on foot. His path will take him over Lendal Bridge, past the Octagonal Tower—the last of the Roman Defences—and St. Mary's Abbey, to the Minster.

York Minster: a great Gothic Cathedral

A Gothic Cathedral is best seen rising from close-knit houses around its base—the Minster is no exception.

'Heart' of York in West Window

The West Front of York Minster is ornate and decorated. You can see the famous Heart of York in the West Window which was restored by monies given by the City of Bradford. The Nave was built between 1300 and 1330, but the two Towers were added in 1472 and the eight pinnacles which surmount these have recently been renewed. Deangate, the road leading round the south side of the Minster which we will follow, was cut in the early 20th century to assist traffic circulation in the City of York.

Now the pressure of traffic makes us wish that Deangate could be closed as recommended in the Esher report.

Strong Buttresses Support West Front

Looking up, one sees the remainder of the finely modelled West Front with strong buttresses capped with gables in each stage, filled with sculpture, and the vertical tracery ornament, all surmounted by the Tower with the pierced parapet and superb pinnacles above, the projecting gargoyles crisp against a brilliant June sky.

Intricate detail on West Front

Standing back from the West Front one looks at the marvellous intricate detail together with the strong buttresses which support the weight of the Towers and which were added later. The persons in the foreground give a clue to the immense size of the Minster.

The Western Doorway

The Western Doorway to the minster is ornate and contains some of the earliest nodding niches in Britain. It was restored in the 19th century but since then due to heavy pollution the stone has decayed further. The restored statues on the left and right are of the Percy Family and the Vavasour Family, both generous donors to the Minster.

Minster's massive size dominates skyline

The size of the Minster can only be appreciated when people are seen around its base. Compared with other buildings it is of stupendous size. Small buildings which flank it such as St Michael-le-Belfry emphasise its size. The photograph shows the south-west corner, the flanking buttresses and the South Transept.

Sculptural quality of ornate Western Towers

From the same viewpoint, glance up at the magnificently ornate Western Towers rising above the 14th century Nave and West Front. The modelling of the ornament and strong relief can be appreciated in this photograph which shows the sculptural quality of the architecture.

South Transept built by Archbishop Walter de Gray

Following the circuit round the Minster one looks back and gets a good view of the whole of the South Transept built by Archbishop Walter de Gray who died in 1256 and is buried in its Eastern Aisle under a magnificent canopy of Purbeck Marble. In the foreground you can see the new trees that have been planted as part of a scheme for improving the precincts of the Minster and the grass which has replaced a tarmac road and parked cars. These improvements are the first implementation of the Esher Report.

250 years work for 20 master masons

Standing further back and going into the grounds of the Song School one gets a magnificent view of the whole of York Minster stretching from the East End, the Central Tower, the Transepts and the Western Towers. This creation of stone and glass containing thrust and counter-thrust took 250 years to build under the direction of at least 20 Master Masons.

There must have been a master plan to achieve such a great work. Full size setting out was done in the "monks' chamber" above the Chapter house vestibule, where accurate details of window tracery have been found.

The famous Rose of York window

Looking up, one sees the magnificent dogtooth ornament in the window of the South Transept—the famous circular window known as the Rose of York. This window has 24 spokes and was restored by the Freemasons of Great Britain in memory of the 11th Earl of Scarbrough who was their Grand Master and the first High Steward of York Minster. Behind the gable of the Transept rises the massive Central Tower to a height of 208ft.

Early English South Transept

Proceeding along Deangate one comes to the pedestrian crossing which leads to the Southern Door which is the climax of a route leading up Stonegate and which marks the line of an ancient Roman Road. This Roman Road was on the central axis of the Roman Legionary Headquarters; and some 12ft. below the group of persons on these steps lie Roman remains which probably saw the day that Constantine was proclaimed Emperor of Rome in A.D. 300. The South Transept was started in 1220 and the detail is bold and crisp Early English, but the doorway is the restoration work of a famous Victorian architect, Edmund Street.

The East Window: John Thornton's masterpiece

Following the circuit one comes to the magnificent East End which is dominated by the Alpha and Omega Window and which was restored by the City of Leeds. Recently the landscaping has been opened up in accordance with the Esher Plan and one sees people enjoying the pleasures of the grass in front of the Minster. The Renaissance Sun Dial in the foreground was set up by the late Dean Milner-White. The East Window is the largest Gothic window in the world, roughly the same dimensions as a single tennis court, and filled with priceless glass by John Thornton of Coventry —put in in 1405-7.

The Chapter House

The Chapter House itself deserves a special study. Recent researches have shown that it was first completed about 1260; but shortly afterwards it was rebuilt and the walls were raised and the buttresses extended. This accounts for the curious design of buttresses with diagonal members surmounted by the more ornate pinnacles. A close study of the masonry after washing shows convincingly the history of events. It is presumed that the first vault fell and that at the second attempt it was decided to dispense with a central pillar and construct a roof of oak trusses. This is one of the most remarkable pieces of early medieval carpentry in Britain and is still standing intact.
There is a model of the roof structure, the work of R. Littlewood, inside the Chapter House.

Central Tower dominates the whole Minster

From Dean's Park one gets a view of the massive Central Tower of the Minster dominating the whole building, but the famous Five Sisters Windows are no less memorable. They are the largest lancet windows in Britain, being about 50 ft. tall and 5' 6" wide, filled with fascinating grisaille glass which is best seen on a May or June evening, when the sun is at right angles to the plane of the glass.

Weight of the Central Tower

On the north side one can appreciate the weight of the Central Tower and the flying buttresses which support the Nave clerestory and the pinnacles which divert the thrusts down into the soil. Since the restoration work this area has been cleaned up, re-sown with grass seed and the road which divided the area reduced to a simple footpath paved with York stone.

Taking optical plumb

To record and monitor the movements of the East Wall two optical plumbs were set up. Here George Preston the Contract Manager is seen setting it up preparatory to making measurements on a permanent brass scale fixed to the floor.

Taking Demec Gauge Measurements

Twenty measuring points were selected, and as occasion arose further points were added. Measurements were taken by George Thompson a Minster Mason at weekly intervals. These were necessary not only to monitor the movements but to guarantee public safety. Three points A, B and C are measured to the centre of the stainless steel dot glued to the stone. The Demec is a Dial Micrometer measuring to 1/10,000 of an inch. It has a personal factor so one only of the masons was entrusted with the task of measurement.

Crack in the Central Tower

The gap shows the total movement but the crack has been superficially filled with mortar which has recently opened about 3/16th": below the masons have pieced in new masonry leaving polythene tubes ready to fill the void behind the crack with liquid mortar (grout). This crack can be attributed to the failure of the foundations over 100 feet below.

Crack below the cill of the East End Window

The story is similar time and again—the cracks have been repointed with mortar only to open out. Some 50 years ago the masons had replaced these three heads with carved replicas only for the stone to be cracked by the movement of the wall due to the faulty foundation below. These cracks were active; six telltales in this area broke in one week.

Deformation

The foundation material at the East End was poor, and it was clear that the pier on the left hand side of the photograph had settled considerably more than that on the right, thus inducing the deformations in the Gothic tracery which are clearly shown in the photograph. Cracks were also visible and these have been pointed in the past but re-opened again. Glass telltales were fixed, and six telltales broke in one week causing some concern. It is also interesting to note the amount of dirt that is deposited on the horizontal surfaces of the Minster. This has now all been removed.

Investigation of Choir Piers

The Choir suffered from a fire in 1829. It was quickly repaired with stone full of 'quarry sap'. The shrinkage of the stone was the true explanation of this and other similar cracks which were noted as being 'old'.

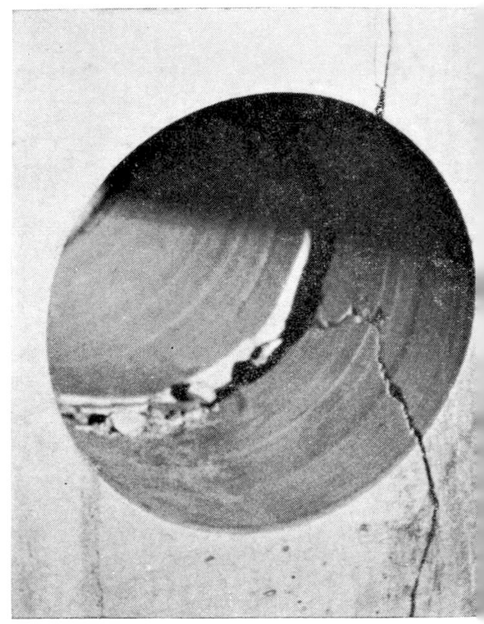

Choir Piers

There were vertical cracks in many of the choir piers. Close investigation showed that these were old cracks as dust had settled, whereas the cracks in the main piers were new, i.e. had no dust. Nevertheless there was no clear reason why these piers should have cracked; so it was decided to strap them as shown in the photograph. Telltales did not break, and an investigation of the history of the Minster suggested that this masonry had been renewed very quickly after the fire of 1829. Further investigation brought to light the fact that fresh stone tends to shrink, and when a core was taken out of the shaft it was found that these cracks did not penetrate more than the thickness of the Victorian facing stone and that the stone behind was solid ashlar and in good condition. It was therefore decided to do nothing about these long vertical cracks as the cause of the trouble had been found and was not likely to re-occur.

Exploration (Central Tower)

Initially a large area was opened up to a depth of 6 feet and secured with planking and strutting and then small areas were dug down to 14 feet depth. Ancient burials of medieval times were removed carefully and reburied with reverence.
It became obvious that the large number of burials had reduced the amount of lateral support to the weak Norman masonry that might have been available from this overburden. A curious white fungus identified as Cephalothecium appeared but soon disappeared.
The planking and strutting was designed to resist the danger of the Norman masonry bursting outwards under pressure from the heavy loads above.

Investigation (Central Tower)

A full investigation was necessary and the foundations of the Norman Minster which carried the Central Tower had to be exposed a small part of the time. It was found that the Normans had used a grillage of oak beams to reinforce their foundations and that by and large this grillage had rotted away leaving voids.
As the photograph shows, these voids were continuous and in fact ran from below the High Altar nearly to the West End. Under the Central Tower the masonry had bent with the settlement but luckily none of these voids had collapsed.

Removing the old beams

Although mostly rotted away, some very tough old oak remained. Wherever possible this was pulled out as it was extremely difficult to drill through.
Structurally this method of strengthening foundations was interesting. If the water table had not fallen it need not have rotted.
Archaeologically the timbers are important, being some of the oldest in Britain. The best sample was preserved for display in the Undercroft.

Planking and Strutting

Planking and strutting follows excavation quickly. This was heavy steel designed to contain the masonry and support a floor above. The detail shows the special high tensile steel bolts used to tighten up the strutting. The planking is 2" thick, with the benefit of experience it should have been treated with the timber preservative, as some of it had to remain in position over three years in damp and poorly ventilated positions; later it became affected by 'rot' and had to be renewed.

Archaeological Excavation

York Minster is probably one of the most important archaeological sites in the country. Finds such as these drums of fallen masonry can alter our interpretation of a whole epoch of history. The archaeologist needs space, time and money to do his work properly. His work involves careful digging, recording, surveying, cleaning up, photography writing notes, cleaning, sorting and labelling artifacts and finally interpretation.

A devoted team of archaeologists under Derek Phillips worked continuously, often through weekends and sometimes round the clock, to keep ahead of the building programme.

The fallen Roman column was found near this spot and has been re-erected outside the south of the Minster.

Excavation (Nave area)

Following archaeological excavation of sensitive areas, bulk excavation was carried out by Messrs. Shepherds.

This photograph gives a good general idea of the excavation of the Nave area. Top left is the south-west column with high tensile steel strapping for safety. The roof of a covered way through which the public can circulate and from which they can view the work shows on the left side.

Centre left is the excavation which has reached water level. A roman wall shows and some twenty tea chests full of fallen plaster have been removed and sent to Mr. Norman Davey for reconstruction. A hoist is in operation and is filling a skep which runs out on rails to a waiting container. Top right is another hoist serving the Nave South Aisle.

Bottom right is the Nave Altar, nearly above the tomb of St. William of York.

At the same time work was proceeding at the middle and the top of the Tower.

Grouting (pier bases)

Between 9/10,000 gallons of grout was pumped into each pier base, in order to consolidate the masonry. Where it all went we do not know, but later when cutting the passages between each of the main foundations some of this grout was found filling voids left by the decayed Norman timbers as shown.
Further grouting was done during the drilling phases and two grouters were kept continuously busy for over four years. Theirs was responsible work, ensuring that all holes were filled and reinforcement properly embedded.

Sandbagging

There was a danger of 'uplift' in the heavily loaded soil in the zones close to the main piers. Accordingly, only a small area was permitted to be exposed at one time in the exploratory phases. The weight of soil removed had to be reinstated as quickly as possible, and to this end thousands of sand bags were used. The photograph shows the area of the central crossing.

Compression Pad

The lowest element of the new foundation was named the compression pad because it was designed to be pushed down into the earth. The pad was about 2 feet thick and had to be excavated below ground water level which meant pumping. On top of the pad, pairs of Fressynet hydraulic cells were set and these would be supplied individually with fluid from a hand pump which would inflate the cells against the superstructure of concrete foundation. As the superstructure was unlikely to move up the pad would have no option but to go down under the immense forces which could be applied by these hydraulic cells.
The cells were covered with precast concrete slabs to protect them from damage during the next stages of work.

Restoration of Central Tower—general view

This is another view of the problem of the Central Tower showing the concrete pumping operation in process, the work of drilling in the middle, the restoration of the windows on the north side and insertion of rainwater downpipes, whilst below the foundation work was in progress.
It was considered necessary to strengthen the centre of the tower with twelve stainless steel rods on each side in order to restrain possible movement while the foundations were being re-constituted.

Insertion of Steel

This photograph shows the insertion of the $1\frac{1}{4}''$ stainless steel threaded bars through the length of the Central Tower. The bars were in short 15 ft. lengths as longer lengths could not be easily managed at this height. Lengths were joined together with screwed couplers.

Anchorage

The steel bar has been inserted and tightened up. Then tightened up against the anchorage and then grouted. The last operation is cutting out the stone to cover the anchorage. One of the principles of this retoration work was that all such repairs should be invisible.

Foundation Reinforcement

Next a steel cage of reinforcement was fixed in accordance with the Consulting Engineers detailed drawings and based on sophisticated calculations done with the help of a computer.

This reinforcement gives tensile strength to concrete and is mainly concentrated round the sides bottom and top of the foundation. In the centre are spiral duct tubes placed so as to save later drilling work in making holes for the stainless steel rods.

Len Gibson is putting the finishing touches to some of the top level steel and it is standing inside the foundation close to the outer shuttering which must be very strong to hold the masses of wet concrete firmly in position.

Pumping

All the $7\frac{1}{2}$/8,000 tons of concrete used in the works was brought ready mixed to the site and most of it was then pumped to where required.

Here Bill Sorby and Dave Whitehead are placing concrete in the first of the foundations to the N.W. Tower. They have to work hard to keep up with a continuous supply of wet concrete which has to be exactly the right mix. Test cubes are taken and crushed at 7 and 28 days to ensure that they are up to standard and strong. No bad results were obtained.

This gang laid 300 cubic yards of concrete in one day—possibly a British record—certainly a tribute to their muscle and the good backing up organisation of Messrs. Shepherd.

Collar Reinforcement

After the massive foundations had been cast the process of fixing steel and shuttering was repeated to form the collars. Starter bars had been left to connect this steel with that of the lower foundations.

The collars were regarded as important as they strengthened and supported the old Norman walls which over nine centuries had carried first a Norman Tower, then after reduction in size an Early English Campanile or bell tower which had fallen and then the even heavier Central Tower, suffering total settlements of up to 14" in the process. Inspection and telltales had shown that there was a tendency for this masonry to burst outwards, so it was considered advisable to contain it with the steel and concrete shown above.

Supervision and Cracks

The movement of all cracks was monitored, but it was found that there could be a time lag of up to six months between the movement of a main pier and an abutting wall such as this on the West Clerestory of the North Transept.

In the photograph can be seen a whole series of diagonal cracks related to the downward movement of the Central Tower being checked by Ken Stephens.

Underpinning the Screen

Underpinning was necessary in order to insert the new foundations, but what a delicate job to support all these Kings, the Kings of England from William the Conqueror to Henry VI! Stage by stage each step was accomplished in congested and difficult circumstances.

The Kings to their credit stayed unmoved, keeping their fixed expressions. Perhaps they were glad to be seen again after having been boxed in for three years by protective plywood.

Drilling

Drilling to start with was a disheartening process. Everything depended upon getting the holes through at two levels in each direction so that the stainless steel rods could be inserted to bond new and old work together.

But after six months only eight holes had been drilled. After trial and error the right equipment was found—a down the hole 'vole hammer' with rotary percussive action and a stiff stem to help accuracy. It was an anxious time with the Central Tower moving downwards. After a conference when all alternative designs that had initially been examined were reviewed, it was agreed that we had chosen the best solution. Therefore as we could not change the design we all had to grin and bear it.

Drillers

The drillers solved the problem and in the end could drill a 'good' hole in two hours or a 'bad' one in eight. However, some holes had to be drilled and re-drilled eight times in order to reach the minimum required standard of accuracy.
600 cu. ft. minimum of air was supplied by a 160 h.p. electric compressor which was totally enclosed so that drilling could go on all night if necessary. Heavier drilling equipment was purchased and gave best results in terms of speed and accuracy. (See left).
Accurate drilling horizontally in masonry is difficult enough but when this masonry is of dubious quality and broken up by centuries of movement, and also has lumps of wood as additional hazards, the difficulties can be appreciated. Diamond core bits were used for accuracy in broken up stone and augers ploughed their way through the wood. The drillers learned all the wrinkles of the job and we owe them a great debt of gratitude.
The drillers worked two shifts for most of the time. They stood for hours in water listening to the groaning of the machines through ear muffs. The machines had to be set up dead accurately in order to hit their target some 50 feet away within limits of tolerance allowed by the Consulting Engineers.

The Halle in B Major

The minster serves as a concert hall, and continued to do so despite the restoration work, which in fact with good planning was not unduly put out by these musical events.
Besides the orchestra, choir and audience you can see the elegant scaffolding for the Central Tower, the Scando hoist and the polythene casing for the famous organ.

The Drills in E Flat

Whilst orchestras played and choirs sang occasionally, the batteries of drills sounded incessantly. One day Dr. Francis Jackson, the Cathedral Organist, was stopped by the Surveyor who said 'What note are those drills playing?' Instantly and in all seriousness the Organist replied: 'E Flat'. This was the moment when his Sonata on the Re-birth of a Cathedral was conceived.

Pier Foundation

The S.W. pier was the second to have its complete concrete foundations, shown here with its 50 rods drilled from the opposite side. The pier is surrounded by its collar which rests on the foundation which is bonded to the old Norman masonry within the stainless steel rods which have been post tensioned to 30 tons per square inch and then anchored, and after a period of stretching, retensioned and grouted finally so ensuring the unity of old and new work. Below these foundations are the hydraulic cells bearing upon the compression pads. Will the pads move downwards as planned? That is the question and the answer will be provided by the rods supported on tripods which are visible above each foundation.

1. Retro-bit 3″ diameter incorporating $1\frac{5}{8}$″ of Pilot Bit. This bit and assembly is used for the purpose of reaming from $1\frac{5}{8}$″ diameter hole to 3″ diameter by rotary-percussive drilling.

2. Standard 3″ diameter cross type tungsten carbide tipped bit used for drilling in homogeneous material by rotary-percussive means.

3. Purpose made 3″ diameter button bit with protruding tungsten carbide inserts used for drilling in broken ground or ground that yields, also used for drilling through timber reinforcements by rotary-percussive means.

4. Standard button bit, 3″ diameter for drilling in broken ground by rotary-percussive means.

5. Standard holbit $1\frac{1}{4}$″ diameter tungsten carbide tipped, used for short bore holes for grouting purposes by rotary-percussive means.

6. Standard retrobit $1\frac{3}{4}$″ diameter tungsten carbide tipped, used for normal drilling operations by rotary-percussive action.

7. As above but 2″ diameter and ditto.

8. Ditto but $2\frac{1}{2}$″ diameter.

9. Standard holbit $1\frac{1}{2}$″ diameter.

10. Standard retrobit 3″ diameter used for normal drilling by rotary-percussive action.

11. Purpose made retro bit incorporating blind pilot, used for reaming $1\frac{5}{8}$″ diameter hole up to 2″ diameter by rotary-percussive action.

12. Standard drill steel coupler type 408 rope thread for coupling 1″ hex steels for rotary-percussive drilling.

13. Standard coupling showing a rope thread coupler used for rotary-percussive action.

14. Purpose made coupler for use with 1″ hex hollow drill steels, designed to provide accuracy when drilling through broken ground, using 3″ diameter retro cross bits. This type of coupling assembly allows the drill cuttings to pass through internally in suspension and centralises the drill steels at coupling points, ideal for drilling operations 50′ - 70′ horizontally in reasonably sound material.

15. Standard $4\frac{1}{4}$″ x 1″ hex shank and (water swivel) 408 rope thread for rotary-percussive action.

16. Standard 508 rope thread coupling used for coupling $1\frac{1}{4}$″ diameter drill steels for rotary-percussive action.

17. Standard $1\frac{1}{2}$″ diameter lugged shank and 512 rope thread assembly for $1\frac{1}{2}$″ diameter round drill steels for rotary-percussive action.

18. Purpose made reamer coupling 3″ diameter for use with $1\frac{1}{4}$″ diameter drill steels, ideal for drilling operations in cementatious material.

19/20. Standard walran type rotary tungsten carbide tipped winged bit used for rotary drilling in timber and fragmented masonry.

21. Standard Trycon roller bit used for rotary drilling in broken ground or material that yields. This type of bit is employed with diamond tubes.

22. Standard Diamond Crown NX with bevelled wall, grade 10 diamonds used for rotary diamond coring and employed with diamond tubes. This bit cuts through masonry, concrete or steel and recovers its core.

GENERAL
All the above described drill head components and assemblies are powered pneumatically for both rotary and rotary-percussive drilling units.

ADVANTAGES AND DISADVANTAGES
High speed rotary-percussive is the most economical means of drilling, tungsten carbide tipped bits are much cheaper than diamond crowns. This type of drilling is fast, but, demands a homogeneous mass, preferably of like material to provide for accuracy in operations where long holes horizontally are required in masonry.
Diamond Core drilling is rather slower—more costly but under adverse conditions in bad material, is more accurate in maintaining alignment.

Problems in the Choir Crypt

The basic problem was to provide end anchorage for the steel reinforcement. This was particularly complicated in the Choir Crypt area, for part of the old masonry had to be underpinned and excavated in order to get the anchorages in the right place. In the top of the photograph you can see Norman masonry supported on concrete needles resting on a beam on the righthand side of the picture. The needles were inserted in holes formed by diamond coring and then cast in concrete.

Tunnelling

The South-East Pier proved to be the most difficult because there was a large mass of Norman masonry which it seemed pointless to remove, but which prevented the anchorages being located where they were required. Accordingly, it was decided to tunnel through and under this mass, and you see the picture here of the work in progress. There is temporary planking and strutting, and you will notice that some of the props are standard Acrow props and others are hydraulic props. Reinforcing steel has been placed for the floor of the foundation and an upstand left for the wall which will lie in the tunnel. However, due to the depth of the work water has crept in and will have to be pumped out before the concrete can be placed. This tunnel has been left so that the end anchorages of each and every rod can be examined in the future.
If ever necessary the reinforcement can be renewed; but it is hoped that it will last for more than 100 years.

Removal of Temporary Floor

Through all phases of the work the Minster had been kept available for services and the public alike. This was mainly achieved by the use of a temporary floor resting on the steel strutting.
It was a turning point in the progress of the work when this floor was removed to make way for the permanent floor.
The photograph shows the 50 feet square foundation of the N.W. pier, the first to be completed and the way this foundation extends to include the easternmost pier of the Nave. The Nave altar has been moved two bays west of its normal position.

Floor Slab 1

People were puzzled by the coffers. The first section was placed over the Nave floor when it was deemed that the movements of the N.W. and S.W. piers had been sufficiently slowed down. Acrow props support the bearers that support the plywood deck resting on joists. The coffers are set on this flat surface.

Floor Slab II

After the coffers have been placed the steel reinforcement is fixed. The gaps between the coffers are for concrete beams running in each direction. The coffers are there simply to save concrete, but they have an attractive aesthetic effect, giving a ceiling supported on no columns and having a floating feeling as it is impossible to see where it joins the walls. Also the effect of the main piers punching through the ceiling and bearing down on the earth can be imagined. Where the ceiling is near the concrete which gives it support, solid concrete has to be used to overcome shear forces.

In the Nave one can see that the floor has been paved and the altar is nearly back in its original position.

In the North Transept the Minster Masons are at work laying the paving. Steel straps have now been removed from the N.W. and S.W. piers.

Floor Slab III

After the placing of the coffers and the fixing of the steel reinforcement, the concrete floor slab was cast. Work is in progress with one man controlling the concrete which is being pumped by a machine situated externally. The foreman, Bill Sorby, is vibrating the concrete. This is a most skilled job as he must be careful not to touch the reinforcing steel. One man is holding the air supply tube. Two men are standing by to help move the concrete cable. On the left one man is using a shovel to finish the concrete which is tamped into position with the long wooden bar with a handle. The structural floor slab can be seen in its completed stage in the foreground. Note that there is not too much water in the concrete, but enough to enable it to flow smoothly. Bob Rowntree is supervising the work.

The Undercroft

The coffers have been removed leaving the concrete waffle slab. Between each waffle is a groove to house electric light conduit.
The piers punch down through the ceiling sitting on the new foundations which are bonded to the old by the stainless steel tie rods. The end anchorages are irregular due to the difficulty of drilling straight.
In the foreground is a wall of the Roman basilica which Sir Mortimer Wheeler pronounced one of the finest pieces of Roman workmanship he had seen.

Death Watch Beetle

Close inspection of the superstructure of the tower roof had revealed heavy death watch beetle infestation. The ends of the beams had already been repaired once in Victorian times using heavy cast iron brackets which show in the photograph. Since then the attack continued and parts of the timber had become friable as is shown by the joiner in the picture. The beams were drilled and found to be faulty. A search was made for replacement timbers, but none of sufficient size were readily available in England even though the press assisted with advertising our need.

Tower Roof
Above, The temporary steel roof covering also strong enough to lift the old beams out.
Below. New steel beams and roof timbers above old lath and plaster vault.

Removal of Oak Beams

Having investigated the problem thoroughly it was decided that there was no course open but to dismantle William Hindley's medieval roof which had served its purpose for over 500 years, and to build a new one. Sections of the timber which were not heavily attacked by death watch beetle were set aside to make joinery for sale in the Cathedral Shop. A temporary roof was put over the Minster and designed so as to enable the beams to be cut up and removed without undue difficulty. The oak had to be cut into short lengths in order to get it down from the top of the Minster safely.

Ring Beam Reinforcement

The top layer of stone was removed from the Minster and saved for future use, and a reinforced concrete ring beam was inserted to prevent the upper parts of the tower from spreading further. Special rainwater arrangements had to be made and these were incorporated inside the ring beam as the up-standing gulleys show. The rain-water pipes themselves were wrapped with electric tape to prevent freezing.

Pumping concrete to the top of the tower

A special pumping operation was organised. The photograph from the top of the Minster shows the road track that was laid to shorten the pipe run for the pump. It also shows the stone that had been taken down and stored in the works area by the North-West Tower. It was a remarkable feat to pump 90 cubic yards of concrete 200 ft. up in less than one day. This was recognised by a special Cembureau award and mention at the Amsterdam conference of European Architectural Heritage Year.
It was typical of the many uses of sophisticated modern plant devised by Ken Stephens for the efficient restoration of a historic building.

Placing the concrete

Here the same gang are at work again placing the concrete as it comes spouting up 200 ft. Bill Sorby is working the vibrator again and supervising the work. In the foreground is one of the rainwater outlets.

St. Peter and St. Paul

This magnificent boss in the centre of William Hindley's roof is nearly five foot in diameter, made up of parts of three oak trees. The boss was carefully stripped down to the original oak looking for traces of medieval colour, but none was found as it had been restored in the early 19th century. All the cracks and defects were filled as can be seen on the left. St. Paul's sword is missing and the joiner responsible for the work was asked to add a Roman sword which he did in an entirely appropriate design. St. Peter is holding his Keys and the Church, while St. Paul is holding his Epistles and his Sword. The bold simplicity of this late Gothic carving has intrigued many art historians.

Central Tower Restored

This photograph shows the transformation wrought by the restoration of the Central Tower. Above the vault is a new roof, and the vault itself has been treated with preservative and all the timbers carefully overhauled and finally covered with a layer of fire resistant insulation. Three coats of new plaster were applied to copper wire mesh on the underside and finished with a fourth coat on the topside to ensure permanence.

The bosses were stripped and cleaned and then repainted using heraldic red as a background and gilding on the highlights. From this distance they stand out brilliantly and read in a way that was never possible before. In the centre are St. Peter and St. Paul. In the next ring are Bishops and Abbots who have had their croziers restored. Between them are angels holding symbols. In the next ring at the four corners are the symbols of the Evangelists, the eagle of St. Matthew, the winged lion of St. Mark, the winged bull of St. Luke and the angel of St. John. Between each of the symbols of the Evangelists are four sets of three figures making twelve in all. These cause some puzzlement as one of these figures is a two-headed monster. It is thought possible they are meant to depict the 12 apostles and the two headed monster is Judas. The boldness and brilliance of these carved bosses is brought out by the decoration.

Carver, Brian West, replacing angel's head

It was found that the heads of two angels were missing and it was desirable that they should be replaced. The aim of the replacement is not to copy medieval work exactly as this would be false, but to provide a modern equivalent. Here Brian West is putting the finishing touches to the head which he has added by glueing and doweling to the original medieval work. In a discreet place the date of his work is scratched so that future art historians need not be misled. The aim is to define the architectural problem and then give the carver a free hand so that his work has vitality.

Erecting Shoring I

Having inspected the foundations from a trial hole it was decided without hesitation that the East End should be shored, but no ordinary shoring was required and special precautions had to be taken in order not to damage the fabric due to thermal movement. These shores each rest on four hydraulic cells which expand and contract with the thermal movements in such a way as to apply a constant horizontal force to the Minster. This avoids local damage and pinching and cracking of stone as well as displacement of vaults. In this picture the first scaffold is being erected. The erection of the scaffolding allayed the fears of the public, particularly the parents of children at the Junior School adjacent, who were deeply concerned for the safety of their children, fearing another Aberfan.

Erecting Shoring II

This photograph shows the delicate problems of co-ordinating two cranes in placing a heavy steel shore without damage to the delicate fabric of the Minster.

Shoring—general view

With the shoring of the East End complete immediate anxiety may have been allayed, but the problem of executing the work remained. The first consideration was the extremely precious glass by John Thornton of Coventry in the Great East Window, which itself is as large as a tennis court. It is the sheer size of things at York Minster that 'gets you'. The size of the window meant that removal for safety was prohibitively expensive and would also have caused some damage to the glass which had only been put in some ten years previously. Accordingly we had to strut the East wall laterally in order to make sure that no deformation occurred, and three horizontal flying shores were placed between the heavy raking shores supporting the East Window. If the East End moved during the works it was essential that the whole wall should move as one and not cause further cracking with the danger of damaging the glass.

Working underground

It was deemed possible to underpin the East End and a careful programme was arranged for inserting 4 ft. lengths of new foundation. Defective old stonework which was not even laid in mortar was removed, and this photograph shows the planking and strutting necessary to hold the wall up and give access to the concretors for their work.

Delivering concrete

Ready mixed concrete was delivered and shot direct into position. Besides the concrete lorry the photograph shows the raking shore, the permanent roof over the excavation and in the foreground is lying reinforcement steel and some of the strutting used in the work. The permanent shelter saved many times its cost as men did not have to be laid off for wet weather.

Concrete Castellation

The castellation is 4 ft. wide, 18 ft. deep and about 9 ft. high. With the experience gained later we might well have arranged for these castellations to be pressurised with hydraulic jacks. As it was, a simple solution was adopted but a certain amount of settlement inevitably resulted. The recess in the side of the castellation is to key it into the next piece of concrete. The programme of casting the castellations was very carefully arranged by the Consulting Engineers so as to avoid any distortions to the East wall and they were successful.

Visual Bend in Wall

The Surveyor's visual inspection had already recorded that the East end Gallery was bending outwards, but when scaffolding was erected it was found that the total bulge on the window above this point was of the order of 9". It is a remarkable fact that stonemasonry is so flexible.

Wire Reinforcement

As mentioned the tracery of the East Window was bulging out and this seemed rather precarious, particularly as the wall itself was leaning 25". Dozens of schemes of strengthening the masonry were discussed, most were expensive and none seemed very effective except the one finally adopted. This solution is a "semi-permanent" one as it is visible. However, the use of wires was tested for three months before the proposal was adopted, and as none of the regular users of the Minster noticed the wires it was felt that they were not too intrusive. These wires restrain the tracery at the node points where it is strongest and will prevent the window being sucked outwards by wind pressure. The solution has the merit of being the cheapest and most effective in spite of being visible.

Techniques—grouting to Western Tower

The picture shows the operatives injecting under a pressure of about 30 lbs. per square inch from a hand pump a mixture of lime cement and flyash with a strength of about $2\frac{1}{2}$ thousand p.s.i. This cementacious mixture is pushed under pressure into the cracks and fissures of the masonry. In some places up to 50 gallons is received through one hole. The procedure is first to drill a hole for the probe, than insert the probe with caulking and point any obvious cracks, then wash the crack out with water. This process dampens the masonry and gives an indication of the amount of grout that will be received. The mixture is adjusted for the amount so that for large volumes a weaker mixture can be used. Lastly, as shown on the photograph, the grout is injected. It may creep out of the cracks, and in the picture you can see the crack above the operative has been caulked with tow. Where the grout comes out it must be cut back and replaced with lime mortar. Some grout may run down the face of the building, and this has to be washed off. The grouters work up the face of the wall and generally it is found that more grout was received in the lower parts of the upper parts.

Coring

The diamond core almost became one of our secret weapons. Initially it was purchased for taking out pellets of stone in preparation for anchorages for the stainless steel rod inserts. Later it came to be used for drilling stone in order to insert needles, and many other useful jobs were found for this somewhat curious looking piece of plant which consists of a hollow drum with diamond teeth powered by a compressed air motor, mounted on a portable stand as shown in the picture. The two operatives are Phil Popley and Paul Heath.

A Troublesome Crack

The independent north-east pier of the South-West Tower presented some unusual problems, as this was found to be badly cracked right through the centre where maximum loads were carried. This pier in fact has some of the heaviest loadings in the Minster, being stressed at 60 tons per sq. ft. As the cracks were rather unfriendly it was decided to put the collar round the masonry below the pier as a matter of urgency, thus reversing the normal procedure of putting the foundation in before the collar. The picture shows the crack, the strutting and some polythene pipe used for injecting grout.

Restoration of the South-West Tower

The South-West Tower is immediately adjacent to Deangate and this raised difficult problems of obtaining working space. Ken Stephens, with the agreement of the City Engineer, arranged for Deangate to be closed from Saturday night until Monday morning, and planned a highly organised operation for excavating under the road and inserting precast concrete beams and slabs in order to provide the working space necessary for the new foundations for the South-West Tower. The photograph shows the first phase of the operation on Saturday when Deangate had been closed and mechanical plant had moved in and started digging the hole for the ground beams. A crane is standing by in the foreground and the precast slabs are laid out ready to be moved into position.

Unfortunately it rained most of the night. On Sunday afternoon you can see Ken Stephens supervising the finish of the job. The precast slabs have been laid in position and the links are being concreted, and soon the road-way will be made good and it will be possible to excavate the working space for the new foundations underneath the protection of this slab whilst traffic runs above at a reduced speed of 10 m.p.h.

Excavation at the West End

By organisation and the use of mechanical plant, every means was used to reduce the cost of the necessarily expensive work of excavation and archaeology. It was decided that conveyors would be the ideal plant for the West End, and here you see the organisation of work of three conveyors converging on one point and discharging out through the West Doors. This is the first phase of excavation and massive lumps of Norman masonry, remains of a Western Tower, have been found; in the lower levels below those being excavated at the moment most important Roman finds were to be found and recorded.

Elevators

The photograph shows the delivery end of the elevators. A series of waste bins were stacked on rollers and filled by the elevators without any manual assistance. When full the waste bin could be pushed laterally on rollers and an empty one moved in. This meant that transport had no wasted standing time. The next thing to note is the total enclosure of the work against wind and rain. This is highly necessary for the comfort of the operatives for good work and for protecting the foundations from inundation.

Archaeology

The photograph shows the archaeologists at work. Derek Phillips is taking levels and Ralph Mills is holding a measuring rod whilst Mary Maddock is recording the measurements and sketching on a drawing. The remains of a post Roman building on the Roman alignment at the West End are being recorded. In the distance three labourers are assisting an archaeologist in an exploratory dig. On the left is part of the main foundation of the South-West Tower and the collar above had been inserted previously. Continuity rods project outwards to bond the next piece of concrete firmly to the existing concrete, and the grooves in the reinforcement are also to assist in securing a good joint. The necessary strutting has been left in position and the concrete poured around it.

Prince Charles' Visit

Prince Charles visited the Minster on December 11th 1970 and it was arranged that he should spend most of his time studying archaeology and the archaeological problems. Here he is talking to Mike Griffiths and is standing in the area being excavated in the last picture.

Foundation Reinforcement

The principles of design of the Western Tower foundations were similar to the Central Tower and relied on drilling. However, there were differences. Firstly, the drilling was at right angles to the masonry. Secondly there were no hazards of embedded timbers and the masonry was in far better condition and there was no difficulty at all about the drilling.

The photograph shows one drilling shot that has gone through concrete, stone and the remaining concrete and come out. The stainless steel rod has been inserted through a polythene lining tube which is exposed by subsequent work. The concrete was left out to be cast later so as to save drilling labours, and the operative is cleaning up the path for one reinforcement rod running parallel to the first. Starter bars are seen projecting from the concrete in the background and at the far right end anchorages of a run of rods is visible. In due course a further buttress of concrete about 2ft. thick and 8ft. high will be cast so as to link the various parts of the foundation together and incorporate the old masonry in a strong girdle of concrete.

Scaffolding temporarily ornaments the Minster

Shoring of the Western Towers

The restoration team were anxious to expedite the work on the Western Towers, but the Minster decided she would not be hustled and said 'No' quietly and firmly when the Western Towers began to move outwards. The shores which had been used for the East End had been kept ready in case such an emergency should arise. These were quickly erected on the same type of pressurised foundations and commissioned. The photograph shows the first shore being placed in position.

The scaffolding of the Western Towers is interesting as work is taking place at three levels with drilling, grouting and washing followed by the Minster masons pointing up and repairing stone. The cleaning of the North-West Tower and centre of the Minster shows up quite vividly.

Traffic was diverted temporarily, and the Dean and Chapter must always be grateful to the City Engineer and the Police for enforcing a 10m.p.h. speed limit and for forbidding the passage of heavy vehicles close to the Minster during the restoration work.

Foundation Failure

The large diagonal cracks in the foundations indicated a major differential settlement due to overloading of the Norman masonary.

Telltales fitted to these cracks were not long in breaking, indicating active movements.

Washing and cleaning the Choir Roof

The encrusted dirt was cleaned off the vaulting and stonework using water, bristle brushes and elbow grease. This was followed by painting with flat oil in an off-white colour and finally gilding the bosses on a background of heraldic red. Only 50% of the area of the boss was covered with gold leaf, but still some 8,000 books of gold leaf were used. Kenneth Clark of 'Civilisation' fame viewed the finished work with the Dean Alan Richardson and pronounced the work both 'artistically and historically correct'.

Cracks I

This photograph is a detail of the cill of a clerestory window at the East End, and shows how old cracks which have been pointed up have re-opened. It also shows the fantastic amount of dirt and encrustation on the internal surfaces of the Minster. These cracks were repointed and regrouted by the Minster masons after the stonework had been washed.

Cracks II

This crack is in the Choir below the triforium gallery on the north side in the bay immediately to the west of the choir transept. The stonework has been cleaned and the full extent of the cracking is now visible in a way that it was impossible to gauge previously. Although this crack appears serious, its significance is not great and it was simply repaired by using stainless steel dowels, grouting and repointing.

Masonry Repairs—Choir South Aisle—easternmost bay

This photograph gives some idea of the disintegration of the structural arches of the windows adjacent to the East End. The Minster masons are expert at handling problems of repair such as the one that was revealed after the stonework had been cleaned and the mortar joints raked out. New stone is cut in and the whole of the masonry consolidated by pointing. As the cause of the movement should have been removed by the correction of the foundation trouble at the East End it is hoped that no further trouble will occur in this area. It should be mentioned that areas of the vaulting were repaired and that loose ribs were dowelled back securely. None of this trouble was readily apparent before the Minster was washed.

Masonry Repairs—dropped arch

In the nave on the south side in the third bay from the Central Tower one of the arches was found to have dropped and this photograph records its condition, after washing but before repair. Messrs. Shepherd provided shoring and hydraulic jacks. The Minster masons cleaned all the open joints out and the arch was pushed back into position with the hydraulic jacks and the joints reformed by pointing followed by grouting. What might have seemed a major job under some circumstances was taken in the stride of the restoration team.

Reinforcing for defective arch

This arch is above the choir stalls on the north side of the choir arcade to the north-east buttress. The photograph shows an interesting case of preventative structural work. It should be noted that the arch has dropped and will need a considerable amount of rectification. However, as the Minster masons were fully extended it was not expedient to carry out this work and temporary measures were taken for the safety of the public and the fabric. The strapping of the north-east pier is also visible.

The photograph shows the Choir all clean, and by way of contrast, the darkness of the uncleaned Nave and Choir North Aisle. There is a considerable amount of displacement of the masonry in the Choir North Aisle which was dealt with at a later date. The Surveyor and the Resident Engineer have to keep these problems under constant review in order to ensure the safety of the public.

Displaced Rib

Regular inspections were made to avoid danger to the public, and fan boards were put where it was considered necessary to provide protection.

In several places in the Minster displaced ribs and cracked masonry were found. This photograph shows a very loose voussoir in the vaulting. The rib had to be taken down and rebuilt together with a sizeable section of vaulting.

Masonry Repairs—dropped voussoir

This photograph shows some of the old and some of the new deformations in the bay adjoining the North-West Tower. The vaulting is cracked, the voussoirs have dropped, some patching is evident, some fresh cracking has occurred and one or two stones are split. It was decided to take down this section of vault and rebuild the ribs and relay the vault. This work was carried out by the Minster masons.

Cleaning the Choir

The dirty and flaking ceiling, the general dullness, the undue contrast between the dark walls and the brilliant windows, the thick layers of dirt obscuring detail and the general air of neglect need no comment as they have all gone.

The Choir before cleaning

This photograph gives some idea of the scale of the operation. The working area at the top of the scaffolding is the same that appeared in the last photograph, and again the contrast between the clean and the dirty is readily visible, and the pattern staining on the dirty ceiling is an indication that the roof should be insulated—which has been done. After the three bays at the East End had been cleaned it was agreed with enthusiasm that the Choir chould be completed provided the contractors could do it by October 17th as there was a wedding on the 18th. This target was achieved. Relics of earlier ages can be seen in the neat gas jets lining the cill of the triforium gallery. It must be admitted that the scaffolded structure has a certain elegance of its own.

Choir Cleaning—after

The lightness and joy of the clean Minster reveals it in a new beauty. This is the way the builders conceived it. The previous Archbishop of York, now Canterbury, came and saw the Choir cleaned and said to the Dean, "You now have a building that will enable you to carry the ministry of God's word further."

Restoration of a Roman Column

The Dean and Chapter presented a Roman Column that had been found in the South Transept to the Civic Trust, but re-erection presented problems, as the Column was badly damaged during its fall and would certainly not stand with safety. The missing defective stone had to be built up to its original contours, and this was effected by forming a stainless steel armature as shown and casting epoxy resin concrete around and finishing with an epoxy resin mixture which simulates stone almost exactly. In the picture you can see the mould for the Column the original fragment with the armature and the carpenter working out the shuttering for the Column base. The Column was re-erected by the Civic Trust on the south side of the Minster in exactly the same order of stones as when it fell. Some people have criticised the lack of entasis but what has been done is archaeologically correct. It is possible that the Column was re-erected in Saxon times and they may have got the entasis wrong.

The Restored Roman Column

The column is here shown in position on the south side of the Minster and floodlit.

Engravings from "The History and Antiquities of the Metropolitical Church of York" by John Britton.

These are the only architecturally accurate drawings of the Minster made before the extensive reconstructions after the fires of 1829 and 1840. They were originally published in 1819 and reissued in 1836.

The examples on page 132 show compartments of the nave, a section across both transepts, the west end, and compartments of the choir, page 133 show sections and elevations of the east end and the end of the north transept, and interior and exterior comparments of the south transept and the chapter house and its vestibules.

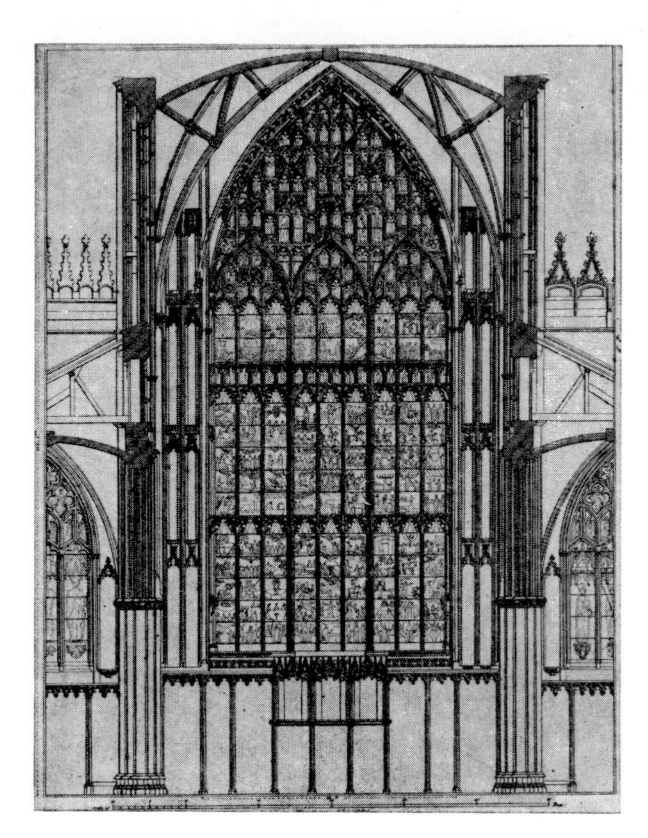

Undercroft I—S.W. Chamber

Remains of the Roman Headquarters basilica stand in the foreground. Behind is the new 50 ft. square foundation of the S.W. Tower pier showing the nuts and bolts of the job. Top left are measuring points and behind part of the 1080 Norman Cathedral shows with its original plaster casing. The whole history of the site is revealed in the Undercroft display.
The work on the Undercroft was made possible by gifts from the Wolfson Foundation and Esme Fairburn Trust.

Undercroft III—North Chamber under North Transept

The history of the site is unfolded in chronological order Roman Saxon and Norman. The magnificent well is part of the 1080 structure whilst the bosses come from the North Transept Roof c. 1250 and the eroded sculptures from the West Front c. 1330.

Undercroft II—West Chamber under Nave

The back wall of the Roman basilica was in good preservation but had to be damp-proofed for it is standing in water. During the excavation twenty two tea chests were filled with mud containing plaster fragments which were skilfully restored by Norman Davey O.B.E. and re-erected as near as possible to their original site.
The coffered ceiling is designed to float visually whilst the main piers pierce it to stand firmly on their new enlarged foundations.

Undercroft IV—Treasury under Choir

This area was excavated in the 1829 restoration work after the Choir was burnt down—but deeper digging needed for the new foundations revealed parts of the Roman Commandant's house. The arch above is suspended to avoid damage to the archaeological remains. This area has been turned into a Treasury through a gift of the Goldsmiths' Company, and houses treasures from Yorkshire Churches and the collection given by Mr William Lee.